RISING
WATER

OTHER BOOKS BY ALPHABET PUBLISHING

Integrated Skills Through Drama

Her Own Worst Enemy
A serious comedy about choosing a career
Alice Savage

Only the Best Intentions
A modern romance between a guy, a girl, and a game
Alice Savage

Rising Water
A stormy drama about being out of control
Alice Savage

The *Fortune* Series

Written and filmed especially for the English language classroom, Fortune is a six-episode action-adventure series and accompanying coursebook that focuses on teaching pragmatics and communication skills. The *Fortune* series is an engaging and motivating alternative to artificial language learning videos or commercial films that lack a learning focus.

Fortune Blue (A2/Elementary+) Student Book and Teacher Book

Fortune Gold (B1/Upper Intermediate) Student Book and Teacher Book

We are a small, independent publishing company that specializes in resources for teachers in the area of English language learning. We believe that a good teacher is resourceful, with a well-stocked toolkit full of ways to elicit, explain, guide, review, encourage, and inspire. We help stock that teacher toolkit by providing teachers with practical, useful, and creative materials.

Sign up for our mailing list on our website, www.alphabetpublishingbooks.com, for announce-ments about new books, and for discounts and giveaways you won't find anywhere else.

All interior artwork licensed from Depositphotos or Adobestock, except as acknowledged below:
South Carolina Air National Guard photo, pg. 18 by Staff Sgt. Daniel J. Martinez, shared under CC BY 2.0 license
Rescue photo, pg. 19 by Texas Military Department, shared under CC BY-ND 2.0 license
Image of Hurricane Harvey by NASA, public domain
Hurricane clean up photo pg. 20 by Alice Savage
Author photo courtesy of Alice Savage.

RISING WATER

ALICE SAVAGE

A Stormy Drama About Being Out of Control

INTEGRATED SKILLS THROUGH DRAMA

Alphabet
PUBLISHING

ISBN: 978-1-948492-14-0 (paperback)
978-1-948492-15-7 (epub)
978-1-948492-16-4 (kindle)

Library of Congress Control Number: 2018945478

Country of Manufacture Specified on the Last Page

First Printing 2018

Published by:
Alphabet Publishing
1204 Main Street #172
Branford, Connecticut 06405 USA

info@alphabetpublishingbooks.com
www.alphabetpublishingbooks.com

Designed by James Arneson Art & Design, JaadBookDesign.com

The author consulted a number of sources while researching the articles and we would like to acknowledge them below:

"Angry Oceans"— "Which Coastal Cities are at Highest Risk of Damaging Floods? New Study Crunches the Numbers." The World Bank, 19 Aug 2013 (http://www.worldbank.org/en/news/feature/2013/08/19/coastal-cities-at-highest-risk-floods); "Record-High Sea Levels along China's Coast 'Could Spell Disaster'." Kinling Lo. South China Morning Post, 23 March 2017 (http://www.scmp.com/news/china/policies-politics/article/2081271/record-high-sea-levels-along-chinas-coast-could-spell); "It's Not Just Harvey: August Marked by Deadly Floods Around World." Madison Park. CNN, 1 Sept. 2017. (https://www.cnn.com/2017/09/01/world/deadly-world-floods/index.html); "The Three-Degree World: The Cities That Will Be Drowned by Global Warming." Josh Holder, Niko Kommenda and Jonathan Watts. The Guardian, 3 Nov. 2017. (https://www.theguardian.com/cities/ng-interactive/2017/nov/03/three-degree-world-cities-drowned-global-warming); "In 2017, the Oceans Were by Far the Hottest Ever Recorded." John Abraham. The Guardian, 26 Jan 2018. (https://www.theguardian.com/environment/climate-consensus-97-per-cent/2018/jan/26/in-2017-the-oceans-were-by-far-the-hottest-ever-recorded); "Syria Signs Paris Agreement - Leaving US Only Country in The World to Refuse Climate Change Deal." Mythili Sampathkumar and Harry Cockburn. The Independent, 7 Nov. 2015. (http://www.independent.co.uk/news/world/middle-east/syria-paris-agreement-us-climate-change-donald-trump-world-country-accord-a8041996.html); "India Cancels Plans for Huge Coal Power Stations as Solar Energy Prices Hit Record Low." Ian Johnston. The Independent, 23 May 2017 (http://www.independent.co.uk/environment/india-solar-power-electricity-cancels-coal-fired-power-stations-record-low-a7751916.html); Project Drawdown's website: http://www.drawdown.org/; "Catastrophic Flooding Could Hit Hong Kong and Macau as Chinese scientists Predict Pearl River Delta May Rise by Over a Metre by End of Century." Stephen Chen. South China Morning Post, 8 March 2018 (

http://www.scmp.com/tech/science-research/article/1858323/sinking-feeling-sea-levels-hong-kong-macau-may-rise-12-metres); "2017 Was the Warmest Year on Record for the Global Ocean." Cheng, L. J., and J. Zhu, Advanced Atmospheric Science, 35(3), 261–263, (https://doi.org/10.1007/s00376-018-8011-z)

"Heroes of the Storm"—"Why Does America Need the Cajun Navy?" Benjamin Wallace-Wells. The New Yorker, 31 Aug. 2017 (https://www.newyorker.com/news/news-desk/why-does-america-need-the-cajun-navy); "Louisiana's 'Cajun Navy' Rooted in its Beginnings During Katrina." ABC13 video of a news broadcast, 28 Aug. 2017. (http://abc13.com/cajun-navy-answers-call-in-harvey-flood-zone/2349668/); "The 'Cajun Navy's' Secret Weapon for Saving Lives: The Human Voice." Peter Holley. The Washington Post, 2 Sept. 2017 (https://www.washingtonpost.com/news/innovations/wp/2017/08/31/the-cajun-navys-secret-weapon-for-saving-lives-the-human-voice/); "I Downloaded an App. And Suddenly, Was Part of the Cajun Navy." Holly Hartman. Chron.com, 22 Dec. 2017 (https://www.chron.com/local/gray-matters/article/I-downloaded-an-app-And-suddenly-I-was-talking-12172506.php); "Harvey. Irma. Maria. Why is this hurricane season so bad?" Angela Fritz. The Washington Post, 23 Sept. 2017. (https://www.washingtonpost.com/news/capital-weather-gang/wp/2017/09/23/harvey-irma-maria-why-is-this-hurricane-season-so-bad/); "Answering the Call: First Responders Reflect on Hurricane Harvey." KHOU. 27 Sept. 2017 (http://www.khou.com/weather/harvey/answering-the-call-first-responders-reflect-on-hurricane-harvey/479151840)

"Teen brain"—"Rates of Motor Vehicle, Crashes, Injuries, and Deaths in Relation to Driver Age, United States, 2014-2015." AAA Research Brief, June 2017 (https://aaafoundation.org/rates-motor-vehicle-crashes-injuries-deaths-relation-driver-age-united-states-2014-2015/); "When Taking Risks is Good for Teens." Jill Suttie. Greater Good Magazine, 26 April 2016. (https://greatergood.berkeley.edu/article/item/when_taking_risks_is_good_for_teens);

Brainstorm: the power and purpose of the teenage brain. Daniel J. Siegel. New York: TarcherPerigee, 2014; "Why It's Time to Lay the Stereotype of the 'Teen Brain' to Rest." Dan Romer. The Conversation, 29 Oct 2017 (https://theconversation.com/why-its-time-to-lay-the-stereotype-of-the-teen-brain-to-rest-85888); "Beyond Stereotypes of Adolescent Risk Taking: Placing the Adolescent Brain in Developmental Context." Daniel Romer, Valerie F. Reyna, and Theodore D. Satterthwaite. Developmental Cognitive Neuroscience, Vol. 27, Oct. 2017 (https://doi.org/10.1016/j.dcn.2017.07.007)

Thank you to my family for loving theatre, especially Cyrus and Kaveh Shafiei because you remind me how much I love it, too. Also, Jorj for keeping on keeping on.

I also want to thank the Carnegie Theatre thespians, Director Steward Savage for making me think about the value of background research, and the Carnegie acting students for helping to workshop the script through readings and recordings. Cyrus, Jackson, Kaveh, Sadie, Shini, and Viviana, as well as Davis, Sam, Scott, and Zander. You showed up and worked hard!

I am also extremely grateful to my colleagues at Lone Star College for believing in me, and for their feedback on the material. Thanks Amy, Anne, Colin, David, Erin, Janet, Joy, Katie, Macarena, Masoud, Ruth, and Cathy. You are all gifted teachers, and I love working with you!

Finally, I want to thank Ken Wilson for your wise counsel and Walton Burns for taking a chance on an unconventional manuscript. It has been a pleasure!

—A.S..

Contents

Introduction

The language classroom is a great place for drama. When you produce a play, you combine both language and skills practice. You study vocabulary, grammar, and pronunciation. You also study conversations and develop strategies for interacting with others. Plays can demonstrate the phrases and expressions we use when we make friends, express frustration, praise talent, and reach other conversational goals.

In this book, you will have a chance to work on all these skills by preparing and performing a play. Through background readings and discussions, you will develop your vocabulary and explore the themes of the play. Through focused stress, intonation, and pronunciation work, you will learn to communicate the emotional intentions of your message, as well as learn the sounds of words in connected speech. Finally, through the production of a play, you will experience

culture and the expressive language in the context of a thrilling story that explores how people behave in a crisis.

A special feature of this book is the opportunity to work on something called **pragmatics**. Pragmatics describes the skill of achieving communicative goals through the culturally appropriate use of language and gesture. Everyone has pragmatics skills in their own language, but it is practiced in different ways among different communities. When people are good at the pragmatics of a language, they reach their goals without hurting their relationships. Here is an example:

Mike lives alone. He would like an invitation to a holiday dinner from his friend Lin. Mike says to Lin, "What are you doing for Thanksgiving?" Lin explains that she and her husband are having a few relatives over. "Oh, that sounds nice," says Mike. There is a pause. Lin says, "What are you doing for the holiday?" and Mike says, "Oh, nothing." There is another pause. Lin says, "Well, why don't come to our house? It's a simple gathering, but we'd love to have you." Mike is happy, "Oh, great!" he says, "Thank you so much. That's very kind of you!" and the conversation continues.

In this short exchange, Mike communicates his desire for an invitation indirectly. Mike cannot say, "Can I come to your house for Thanksgiving?" because that would not be polite. He would be putting Lin in an awkward position because it would be hard for her to say no. Instead, Mike creates the conditions for Lin to understand his situation. Then *she* can decide to invite him or not without feeling uncomfortable or rude.

In this instance, Mike is demonstrating good social skills, which is another way of saying he's good at pragmatics. However, this is only true if Lin is happy with the conversation as well. If Lin feels that Mike has pushed her to make the offer, she will use her own pragmatics skills to let him know that his efforts to get an invitation were inappropriate.

Pragmatics skills are most useful in challenging situations. These situations rarely appear in textbooks, which is why pragmatics is often considered a hidden language. In fact, people tend to need pragmatics most during uncomfortable or important conversations. In these cases, people with good pragmatics skills use special phrases to signal their intention. For example, look at the sentence, "I don't want you to take this the wrong way, but I don't think singing is for you."

The expression, *I don't want you to take this wrong way, but . . .* is a familiar signal in English. It helps you warn someone that you are going to say something that is truthful, but not complimentary. When the listener knows criticism is coming, they can prepare for it. There are many of these signal phrases that you can use to feel in control of a conversation. A play is a good place to learn them because you can experience the expressions in a social and emotional context.

In addition to pragmatics, you will have opportunities to practice the more familiar skills of pronunciation. You can develop a natural tone, effective intonation, and even use gestures because you will be speaking high frequency phrases in contexts typically used by family members and friends. You may notice that your voice goes up or down, or slower or faster, depending on the mood of your character. Sometimes you will try to speak in a joking way. At other times, you will show frustration or confusion.

Sentence and word stress will also be important. As you rehearse, you must make decisions about which content words to emphasize. You'll say these words louder and clearer, so the audience will understand. You'll also become aware of syllable stress in longer words. Having the right syllable stress is one of the most important features for comprehensibility.

Furthermore, the pronunciation and intonation work of the rehearsal stage is valuable because you are working with language in a social and emotional context. Not only *what* you say but also *how* you say it is important because the delivery will have an effect on your relationships with other characters. A first reading often begins with actors speaking in a dull monotone. As you progress with pronunciation, stress, and intonation, however, you may be surprised at how much personality is communicated through the sound of your voice.

Producing a play is more than just practicing with someone else's words, however. It also involves doing background research into your character and working with others to tell a story in a way that reflects your ideas about the world. Throughout the process, you'll have meaningful discussions about the issues raised by *Rising Water*. This practice will help you become better at longer conversations where you can share opinions, give reasons, clarify your understanding, offer and respond to advice, and provide encouragement to your peers. These are all useful academic and workplace abilities.

Finally, improvisation activities and role-plays can help you build bridges between the world of the play and the world outside the classroom. When you take on a character, you explore a different identity and the choices that person makes. You can pretend to be that character in new situations to explore different choices or simply to have fun "play-ing" with language and context. You can also transfer expressions and choices to new situations by creating original role-plays and even writing your own scenes.

After the play, you will find additional activities for repurposing the content and language in new ways. Hopefully, by the end of this book, you'll feel a little more confident about your English conversational skills, especially when talking about the future of cities, and how we can best prepare ourselves and our communities for the challenges ahead.

How to Use This Book

The activities and ideas in this book are presented in a specific sequence. However, the book is designed to be flexible. You can use it alone or to support a course book. Some teachers may take a month or two to work on the play and the accompanying activities. A longer time frame allows you to go deeper into research and skills development throughout the rehearsal period. Other teachers may take a week, skip over some of the activities, shorten rehearsal time, and have students read with a script in hand. Either way, students working in collaboration can benefit from their experience with conversational English.

The best way to plan your theatre production is to read through the script, activities, and background reading texts. Then decide on an approach that best fits your students' level, your curricular objectives, and your schedule. Also decide how much you will need to be involved in supporting the production. For many classes, the students are able to do much of the work themselves. By putting them in charge, you give them opportunities to use language to share ideas, solve problems, make suggestions, give feedback, and otherwise negotiate meaning in a way that feels purposeful and relevant.

Once you have decided on an approach, you can mix and match the activities to fit your curricular objectives. There are related articles that can be expanded to work on reading skills. There are writing prompts that allow students to analyze the topic from different perspectives. These can also be used as preparation for a mini-debate on whether young people should be given opportunities to take risks—a major theme of *Rising Water*. Some teachers might like to reserve part of the class for skills work and the other part of the class for rehearsal.

To plan the production, think carefully about your schedule. You want students to feel a sense of accomplishment at the end. Having students memorize lines, block, rehearse, and perform a play is rewarding but it takes an investment of time and energy. If you don't have the time, you can aim for a rehearsed reading in the style of Reader's Theater and still reap many of the benefits. (For Reader's Theater support, go to http://www.alphabetpublishingbooks.com/integrated-skills-through-drama.) Readers' theater is particularly effective when your goal is to capture the sounds and rhythm of English.

In terms of leveling, there are a number of ways to adjust the materials to fit the level of your class. This module is designed for intermediate levels and above. For lower levels, you might want to simply use the play as a text. You can do the activities and discuss the characters' decisions and the plot, as well as the topic of human behavior in times of crisis. Then you can have students practice reading the parts from the script to work on sounds and intonation. For middle levels, you might have students memorize and perform the play, but use the intermission model on page [XX] to allow for questions, or let the audience read along. To increase the challenge for higher levels, do a full performance. Have students memorize lines and perform for another group, or even create a video to be shown to a wider audience. Also, feel free to allow students to adapt the script to suit their goals If you have several groups stage the same play, consider small changes such as having a female actor play the male lead, or having some of the groups rewrite a specific scene, such as the ending, or even write new scenes. (In this case, you will want to change names in the script to reflect different genders or countries as needed.) Small adaptations like this will allow you and the students to be creative while keeping the show fresh from one performance to the next. If groups produce different plays, you may want to start performances with a short introduction to the script's central issues. This can be done by the director as a way to help the audience follow the plot. In addition, you can also add or double up roles. It may be helpful to have at least one person who does not act take on the role of director, videographer, and/or stage manager. For more ideas see the suggestions below.

While students are rehearsing, you can circulate, take notes, and provide language and skills support as needed. You can also meet with each group to give specific feedback on pronunciation or scene work. Some groups may need more encouragement than others, but as long as the play is comprehensible, and they have the language skills to communicate with each other, students should be able to produce a play with minimal support.

You also have choices on how you handle performances. Some teachers like to do all the plays on the same day, while others do one a day for two or more days. If your class is doing one play, you might perform for a different class, perhaps one at a lower level. In any case, allow 25 to 30 minutes for each performance and consider doing a talkback or having classmates give feedback at the end. (See the post-performance section)

Finally, there are ideas for different types of assessment at the end of the book. If using a rubric such as the one on page [XX], it is a good idea to give the rubric to the students at the beginning of the production, so they know what you will value. In a real production, the director simply gives notes. These notes tell the student how you felt when they said or did something and sometimes offer suggestions for alternatives. Notes are more supportive and less evaluative. This may be preferable if you do not need to give a specific grade.

Most importantly, enjoy the process! Experiment. Think critically. Be creative. And above all, have fun!

SUGGESTIONS FOR DIFFERENT CLASS SIZES

Different classes have different numbers of students. This can present a challenge when producing a play so here are some suggestions for making sure all students are engaged. By dividing the class into groups and giving each group a project, you can provide practice for everyone. One way to do this is to give students a preference sheet. Some may prefer to act. Others may prefer to participate in a debate.

Group option one: Have each group produce the play but give the production their own unique interpretation. Each group can discuss and adapt the play as they wish. They can combine or cut roles. They can also add scenes as they wish. Groups can perform for each other and discuss their different choices.

Group option two: Produce two different plays by having a second group work with one of the other plays in Alphabet Publishing's *Integrated Skills through Drama* series. Have the two groups perform for each other.

Group option three: Have one group organize and have a debate based on the readings and possibly some outside research on the topic. See suggestions for debate topics on page XX in the post-performance section and find materials for structuring a mini-debate on the Alphabet Publishing website at: http://www.alphabetpublishingbooks.com/integrated-skills-through-drama)

Group option four: Have one or two videographers make a documentary about the process. They can interview and film the actors as they prepare for their roles. Then the videographers can edit the video and share it with the class.

Group option five: Have one group write and produce a short sequel to the play or even a different play around the theme of teenage risk-taking. To get started, they need characters and a conflict that they need to overcome. Choose one of the following ideas or create your own. Create enough characters so that everyone has a role. See page XX in the post-performance section for ideas.

Preview

THINK ABOUT THE TOPIC

Look at the photo and discuss your answers to the questions below:

    a. How would you describe the people in these pictures?
    b. What kind of confidence does each person need?
    c. Which image reflects your personal strengths? How?

DISCUSS THE TITLE

Read the statements with the phrase *out of control* below. Then discuss your answers to the questions with a partner. Share with the class

1. I just got the bill, and our spending is totally *out of control*. We're going to have to cut up the credit card!

    Who is talking?

    Where are they?

    What might have happened?

2. I'm really worried about Natalie's grades, Mrs. Louis. Her screen time has gotten way *out of control* and she won't listen to me or her father. We've tried taking away her phone until she finishes her homework, but she refuses to do it.

Who is talking?

Where are they?

What might have happened?

3. I'm not sure why you are so mad at me. The decision to cancel the project was *out of my control*.

Who is talking?

Where are they?

What might have happened?

The expression *out of control* is used when people cannot manage a person or a situation. Here are some examples.

- Parents often say their children are *out of control* when the children do not obey them or make reckless choices.
- A person can also say, "*It is out of my control,*" when they have no power to influence a decision.
- Sometimes people say a natural disaster is *out of control* when they feel powerless to stop it. For example, "The forest fire is burning out of control," means that the firefighters cannot put out the fire.
- Sometimes people also use the expression *losing control*. This means they are about to become emotional or unable to handle a situation with a person or machine.

CONVERSATION SKILLS

Read the situations below. Work with a partner. Decide what you would you say *to* the person. Then think of what you would say *about* the person to someone else. Try to use the expression *out of control* or *lose control*.

The person is:
- driving their car very fast and dangerously because the person is upset about being late.
- playing soccer or basketball and gets in a fight with someone on the other team.

- going into debt because they are spending a lot of money on entertainment.
- playing computer games so much that they are not taking a shower, stopping for meals, or going to school or work.

WRITE ABOUT THE TOPIC

Sometimes teenagers take risks. They break rules or do dangerous things even when they know they might get in trouble. Social science researchers now want to understand why young people can be reckless. What are your thoughts? Think about the questions below and try to answer them in three or four detailed paragraphs.

- Can you think of a time when you took a risk, as a teenager? Where were you? Who were you with? What did you do? Why did you do it?
- What happened afterwards? What were the positive and negative effects? What did you learn about yourself or the world?
- What do you think teachers, parents, and other adults need to understand about teenagers' need for adventure? And what can they do to support teens?

Share your stories in groups. Who likes taking risks? When is it good to take risks?

READ FOR BACKGROUND

This play explores how different people behave during a natural disaster. To understand the context, it is helpful to do some background reading on the issues.

Vocabulary

Match the phrases from the texts in column 2 to their meanings in column 1. Look up words or expressions that you want to learn more about. Try to use them in new sentences or dialogs in order to remember them.

1. *i* Its goal is to help people, not make money.	a. an iceberg
2. _____ Everyone benefits from the outcome.	b. the accumulation of so much melted ice
3. _____ energy that comes from burning carbon, including coal or gas.	c. The flooding devastated Bangladesh.
4. _____ A lot of ice becomes water.	d. leapfrogging over traditional sources of energy
5. _____ changing from having no energy to using new sources such as wind or solar.	e. small-scale energy projects
6. _____ a very large chunk of ice floating in the ocean.	f. withdrew from the agreement
7. _____ Urban areas are in danger.	g. Businesses can prosper.
8. _____ The country agreed at first and then decided not to participate in a plan.	h. carbon-based energy
9. _____ Companies have the ability to grow and make a lot of money.	i. ~~a non-profit organization~~
10. _____ buildings, streets, power, and water systems that exist in a city	j. a win-win situation
11. _____ a local solution to generating power, might be a solar panel on someone's home	k. vulnerable cities
12. _____ Rising water created a lot of destruction in the country.	l. urban infrastructure

READ the article about the effects of technology on modern families. Highlight and take notes on important points. Then do the discussion task below.

Angry Oceans

In June of 2017, a large section of the Larsen C ice shelf in Antarctica broke off and floated into the ocean. The iceberg was 512 square kilometers, bigger than some countries, but it will not stay that way. Eventually the ice will melt and become seawater. Even at this size, it will not raise sea levels by much, but it is not the only ice that is melting.

Greenland's glaciers (rivers of ice) are similarly breaking off and floating out into the world's oceans, and the sea ice at the North Pole is also rapidly melting. Now there is much more open ocean. The accumulation of so much melted ice is beginning to affect coastlines around the world, threatening many of the world's major cities.

According to a World Bank report published in 2013, rising sea levels will affect major cities along the world's coastlines. The cities of Guangzhou and Shenzhen in China; New York, Miami, and New Orleans in the United States; Nagoya and Osaka in Japan; and Mumbai in India will experience more frequent and dangerous flooding along with the economic and social hardships that come with it. Other vulnerable cities include Ho Chi Minh City in Vietnam, Guayaquil in Ecuador,

Khulna in Bangladesh, and Palembang in Indonesia. Alexandria, Egypt, Naples, Italy, and Rio de Janeiro, Brazil are also in danger. And according to a separate study done at the Chinese Academy of Sciences Institute of Atmospheric Physics (CAS-IAP), the financial and cultural centers of Hong Kong and Macau could face severe flooding by the middle of the century.

It is estimated that the cost of flooding will rise to a trillion dollars by the 2050s, but economics is only one issue. Many of these cities also have historical and cultural value as most older cities were developed at a time when rivers and oceans provided the main form of transportation. Many traditional waterfronts with their unique architecture and culturally distinct neighborhoods are impossible to replace. Shanghai, for example, is famous for The Bund, a historic walkway with colonial buildings and distinctive high rises. On the other side of the world, Rio de Janeiro's Copacabana Beach is a world-famous tourist attraction. Both have a powerful place in the hearts and minds of their citizens but are currently under threat.

Unfortunately, ocean levels may be rising faster than scientists first thought, and this is because the ocean temperature is also rising. A study by Lijing Cheng and Jiang Zhu of CAS-IAP reported that 2017 was the warmest year for oceans on record. In fact, since the beginning of the 20th century, the oceans have been getting steadily warmer, not only at the surface but also deep under the water. This change has consequences. Warm water takes up more space than cold water, which adds to rising sea levels. Warm water also melts ice faster than cold water. The loss of ice, which reflects sunlight, means that the newly melted arctic oceans absorb even more heat, continuing the cycle of rising sea levels and melting ice.

A warmer ocean brings another problem: storms. This is particularly true in the Atlantic Ocean where storms form off the west coast of Africa and can arrive in the North and Central Americas as massive hurricanes. In the fall of 2017, there were more storms and bigger ones than usual. There were sixteen hurricanes, and six were category 3 or higher, which means they had winds of 110 miles per hour or more. Several became famous for the damage they caused. Puerto Rico was especially hard hit as Hurricane Maria went directly over the island and destroyed homes, buildings, and power plants. The island did not have access to electricity or clean water for weeks, and many suffered for months.

On the other side of the world, storms also brought more rain than usual. Flooding devastated Bangladesh, Nepal, and Southern India in the fall of 2017. Millions of people became homeless and over 1,000 died according to the International Federation of Red Cross and Red Crescent Societies. Meanwhile, in South America, unusually severe flooding also affected cities in Peru and Ecuador. In Africa, flooding caused damage and loss of life in Sierra Leone and Nigeria.

To prepare for a wetter future, many leaders are taking steps to reduce the effects of climate change on urban areas. The Paris Climate agreement, which has been signed by all the countries of the world, has a goal of preventing the global temperature from rising more than 2 percent. While the U.S. withdrew from the agreement in 2017, many U.S. states and cities promised to continue working with the international community on climate goals.

Much of that work involves shifting to cleaner sources of energy. China, one of the world's biggest users of carbon-based energy, is becoming a leader in solar. The country has a new slogan, *Make China's Skies Blue Again*, and it has invested heavily in creating solar farms and buildings that can draw power from the sun. India has canceled plans to build new coal plants because solar is not only better for the environment but also cheaper. In the U.S. state of Texas, wind energy is set to produce more power than coal by 2025.

At the World Economic Forum in Davos Switzerland in early 2018, world leaders gathered to discuss ways that businesses can prosper with climate-friendly practices. One goal is to find a way to store energy with the development of new and better batteries. Another goal is to make buildings more efficient. Isabelle Kocher, a businesswoman and leader in a non-profit organization that brings renewable energy to developing countries, talked about how building climate-friendly infrastructure is a win-win situation because it creates loyalty from customers who value sustainability while also creating savings for companies.

And in developing countries, small communities and villages are leapfrogging over traditional sources of energy and going straight to solar and wind energy because it is easier and more afford-able than building a power plant. Visitors to a village in rural Africa or a mountaintop in Ecuador should not be surprised to see shiny solar panels atop traditional homes. These small-scale energy projects allow people to access the Internet and participate in the larger economy without causing pollution.

Investment in education and the development of new technologies and resources are also helping people plan for the future. A non-profit organization called Project Drawdown has posted 100 solutions on their website, and many of them are surprisingly achievable. One is to eat less meat, especially beef. Another is to change the way we make plastic by using more plant-based materials. All of these are indirect behaviors that reduce pollution in the air and water.

Many of these solutions can also improve life for cities, and some are already happening. Cities from Seoul, Korea to Sydney, Australia, to Copenhagen, Denmark to Houston in the American state of Texas are creating greener transportation solutions by building bicycle paths and parkways. Others are planting wetlands or forests to create a protective area between the ocean and urban infrastructure.

Foresters, such as the Japanese teacher, Akira Miyawaki, are helping communities to create tall forests more quickly than trees grow naturally. Forests provide natural beauty, but they do other important jobs as well. Forests clean the air by absorbing carbon, and they can increase rainfall in dry areas. When there is a flood, the tree roots hold on to the land so that it does not wash away. Mangrove forests are particularly effective at providing protection because they can handle salt and fresh water.

Finally, innovative companies are also working on technology that can remove carbon from the atmosphere. While it is currently not cost-effective (This means that it is still very expensive), small-scale projects have shown that carbon removal is possible. In fact, the captured carbon can be used as a new type of fuel, or it can become new products. Feed for animals is just one example.

There is a saying in English, "Where there is a will, there is a way." This saying means that when people have the desire to solve a problem, they can find a solution. Now, at the beginning of the 21st century, citizens around the world are realizing that past human behavior has threatened our future. As sea levels begin to rise, the will to protect cities is gaining strength. Fortunately, we are becoming more innovative and more collaborative in finding a way.

Discussion

1. Do you know of any cities that have floods or other problems related to weather?

2. What solutions for protecting cities do you like? Explain.

3. What would you like your city to look like in 20 or 50 years? Think about transportation, public spaces, and housing.

Insight sentences

Complete the sentences with your own ideas.

1. This reading and discussion made me think more about _____.

2. In thinking about the future, the most important actions we can take are _____

_____ .

Vocabulary

Read the sentences below and discuss the meaning of the expressions.

1. You couldn't really wrap your head around it," said a first responder who helped hundreds of hurricane victims to safety.

   What does *wrap your head around it* mean?

2. "It kind of tugged at my heart," said a volunteer who saved an elderly man who would not leave his home without his pet dog.

   What does *tugged at my heart* mean?

READ the article about how people helped each during a 2017 flood in Houston, Texas. Highlight important points. Then do the discussion task below.

Heroes of the Storm

"We need help."

"We had five elderly people, and only two have been rescued in New Caney."

"I've got a gentleman trapped inside of a black truck. … One male, and one German Shepherd named Happy."

"In Cypresswood, they are needing boats over there. They said they have boats running, but they have about 600 people stranded. We are headed that way … just coming out of Spring."

"Take a picture, write down your address and phone number. Add it to this group and we can get to you."

These calls came to Texas Search and Rescue during Hurricane Harvey in 2017. Over a period of about 72 hours, the storm dropped 50 inches of rain in the greater Houston area (about a trillion gallons). It flooded streets and trapped people in their homes. Some tried to walk out into the flooded streets. Others went to upstairs bedrooms or roofs and used their cell phones to call for help.

Emergency teams worked around the clock to respond to the calls. The Houston police, fire, and traffic safety workers left their families and came to work. They got in small boats and went looking for victims. The water was often so deep that the boats passed over the tops of cars.

"You couldn't really wrap your head around it," an officer told KHOU, a local television station later. "You don't have any control," said another. Many of them also said they could not have done it alone. "We could not have achieved what this city has achieved without all the volunteers," said a third.

Indeed, while government workers responded quickly, they were overwhelmed by the need. Greater Houston is bigger than some states, and water had flooded the roads, so people could not escape. The army came with big trucks. They began moving people out, but the emergency calls kept coming. More help was needed.

That help came. Ordinary citizens with small boats put on their rain gear and went out into the storm with the official emergency crews. They coordinated with volunteer operators who used cell phones and social media to find victims. Then they used GPS systems to drive their boats through flooded neighborhoods. As day turned to night, they kept going back again and again to answer the calls.

Volunteers organize

Many of these volunteers were good at the work. They quickly set up communication systems through social media and an app called Zello. They also knew how to navigate the dangerous water. This coordinated effort came from experience. Many of these people had done it before, not just in Houston, but in other cities where storm floods put people in danger.

One of the largest volunteer groups is called the Cajun Navy. The Cajun Navy is not a government agency. It is a group of fishermen from the neighboring state of Louisiana. They are called Cajuns because they identify with French-speaking Canadian immigrants who came to the U.S. over 200 years ago. These strong and resilient people built homes near the Gulf Coast and learned to live in a difficult environment. Their French history has influenced their music, food, and culture, and they have a strong sense of place. They also have boats, and these boats are made to travel in places where water is not deep.

When Hurricane Katrina devastated the city of New Orleans in 2005, Cajun fishermen were equipped to travel into the flooded city and help victims. As they gained experience and recognition, they took on the name Cajun Navy. When Harvey threatened Houston, many of them remembered how people in Houston had helped them during Katrina. So, they attached their boats to the backs of their trucks and came to help their neighbors.

One of the volunteers was a man named Joshua Lincoln. Lincoln's home had flooded during Katrina. When he heard about Harvey's flood victims, he decided not to go to work. Instead, he took his boat to Houston to help. Later, in an interview with CNN, he said, "Seeing how people in Texas responded and helped us in a disaster kind of tugged at my heart." Lincoln and others were able to help many people, including an unconscious woman who was floating face down in the water. Only their sharp eyes and quick action saved her.

While some rescues happened out-side, much of the danger happened inside homes. People who are caught in rising water have to make difficult choices, and sometimes their decisions increase the danger they are in. One of these choices is whether to go upstairs or try to get up on the roof. The roof is safer when water gets very high, but the upstairs is easier. Many of the most vulnerable victims such as the elderly and families with young chil-dren chose to go upstairs. They could not believe the water would pass the second floor. However, for a few people, it did.

Then they had to make an even harder choice: Go out the window and try to get on the roof or go into their attic.

The attic is the area above the top floor that is often used for storage. Most attics do not have windows, so there is no escape. As flooding increased during Harvey, social media posts became more urgent. "Do not go into your attic," people posted and reposted. Yet first responders were hearing calls from attics where families were trapped. Volunteer phone operators connected the rescuers with people in the most danger. Many of them stayed up all night making sure the victims got help.

Recovery and rebuilding

While big coordinated efforts helped with extreme situations, individuals also helped each other. Along a quiet street in the Houston neighborhood of Bellaire, the Hancock family was asleep when the rain started to fall. In the middle of the night, a neighbor knocked on the door. When Chandel Hancock got up to answer it, her feet splashed into the water that was rising around her bed. Chan-del, her husband, and their son found themselves walking in waist-high water, hopelessly watching as their living room became a lake.

That's when the neighbors stepped up. They brought the wet family into their home, gave them blankets, and made plans to help them clean out the ruined house. One woman took all the Han-cock's wet clothes to her home so she could wash and dry them. Another brought food.

When schools closed in the weeks following the flood, young people put down their phones and picked up tools. With extra time on their hands, thousands of students organized to tear out walls and carry wet furniture to the street alongside the adults. "I'm not doing this to look good on a college application," said a high school senior taking a break from dragging wet carpet to the street. "I'm doing it because I have to. I can't *not* help." And in that way, Houston began its long recovery.

All in all, first responders rescued more than 10,000 people, and in the days after the storm, thousands of ordinary people donated money, clothes, furniture, labor, and whatever else they could to help their neighbors rebuild. Some people cooked meals or ordered pizzas and brought them to strangers who were working on the homes of neighbors they did not know.

In the end, no one wanted the flood to happen, but the lessons of Harvey, Katrina, and the other storms that came before were powerful. When crisis happens, people will be there to help each other.

Discussion

1. What would you do if you woke up and there was water coming into your home?

2. In your opinion, why did so many teenagers and people from other places help?

3. There is a saying in English that "hard times bring out the best in people." Do you agree? Can you give examples from your life?

Insight sentences

1. This text/conversation made me think more about_____
   _____ .

2. People volunteered to help because_____
   _____ .

3. Emergencies cause people to_____
   _____ .

Vocabulary

Circle the letter of the phrase that best completes the sentences. Then discuss the meaning of the sentences. Do you agree or disagree?

1. Some older people may have **rigid ways of thinking,** so they struggle in a creative environment.

   a. creative and open mind

   b. a closed mind

2. It makes sense that most teenagers **crave new experiences** because their brains develop by learning from *doing* things.

   a. feel a strong desire for adventure

   b. dislike things that are different

3. A small percentage of teens **lack impulse control**, and they are more likely to continue bad behavior because they do not think about consequences.

    a. manage sudden desires

    b. act without thinking about possible negative effects

4. Older people are calmer and tend to avoid risk, so they can benefit from younger people's **emotional intensity** and willingness to take a chance on something different.

    a. having few emotions

    b. having strong emotions

5. Teachers, police officers, sports coaches, and other **authority figures** are trained to help teens take risks that do not endanger the teenagers' lives.

    a. adults with power and responsibility

    b. dangerous and difficult jobs

READ the article about how science is now explaining teenagers' relationship with risk. Highlight important points. Then do the discussion task below.

Should We Fear the Teenage Brain?

The skateboard park at Seattle Center was busy on a weekday afternoon. Observers gathered around to watch while a young man in baggy shorts worked on a tricky jump. "Shouldn't he be wearing a helmet?" said a woman carrying a baby. Others nodded in agreement. "That boy is just too reckless!"

The young man did not hear the comments, or he did not care. He continued to throw himself into the air, often coming dangerously close to falling on his head.

Suddenly a little girl of about five got up and approached the skater. The audience watched, afraid, as he came over a jump and headed straight toward her. Suddenly he stopped, flipped up his board, and picked her up.

"I'm hungry," she said.

"Okay. Mom's probably home by now. Let's go get some dinner."

The audience sighed with relief and began to walk away. This 'crazy' teenager was going to live another day.

The image of the risk-taking young athlete who is also a caretaker for his younger sister reveals the mixed views that society has of teenagers. For adults, young people can sometimes seem to be out of control and capable of risking their lives for no clear reason. At other times, they are responsible, caring, and cooperative. Which one describes the real teen?

If we are to believe insurance companies, teens are a danger to themselves and others. Most automobile policies charge extra for teen drivers, especially males. There are also laws to prevent young drivers from having teenage passengers. Statistics support these rules. According to the Automobile Association of America (AAA), teens are responsible for more car crashes than any other age group, and the likelihood of a crash increases when other teens are in the car.

Unfortunately, these statistics often come with tragic accounts of accidents, and the stories spread quickly. As a result, many people in authority fear teenage decision making. They fear that all teens lack impulse control and take risks without thinking about the consequences. Driving is just one example.

However, there is another side to the story. Researchers who study teenage behavior can now use scientific tools to look inside the teenage brain. The results of their work suggest that society should better appreciate the minds of young adults. Perhaps teenagers put themselves in dangerous situations for a reason.

One of these researchers is Daniel Siegel. Dr. Siegel is a psychiatrist and neurobiologist who has written several books about the brain, and he believes that the kids are alright. In fact, he thinks risk-taking is a necessary part of growing up.

Siegel has identified four factors that motivate young people when they take risks. The first is that teenagers crave new experiences. For example, teenagers might climb a neighbor's tree to steal fruit because they want the thrill of danger. The second is social engagement. Teens will enjoy the adventure more if they are with friends because they strengthen relationships through shared experience. The third is emotional intensity. Sneaking into a neighbor's yard and climbing a tree is simply exciting. And finally, teens like creative exploration. The experience of making a secret plan and carrying it out gives young people awareness of how it feels to go against normal behavior. They do not know what it feels like to break rules until they actually do.

While these four factors may alarm parents, they make sense to Siegel who says these experiences provide a path to wisdom and maturity. In his book *Brainstorm: The Power and Purpose of the Teenage Brain*, he says society should support teens in their risk-taking to help them develop self-awareness. Teens need experiences to find out who they are. A young man does not know if he is brave until he jumps off a bridge into a river. A young woman does not know if she is powerful until she speaks up when something is unfair.

Dr. Dan Romer, the Research Director at the Annenberg Public Policy Center of the University of Pennsylvania, would agree. Romer has also done extensive scientific research on the teenage brain, and he also says that the years between 12 and 25 mark an important stage of the brain's development. Like Siegel, he believes the brain's chemistry pushes young people to take risks in a way that prepares their thought processes for later in life. According to Romer, the brain learns best

from experiences. And many of these experiences involve risk because risk lies at the boundary between what is safe and familiar and what is new and different. In other words, the science suggests that without risk, it is difficult to gain experience, and without experience, it is difficult to learn how to make hard choices. If teenagers are prevented from testing themselves against personal challenges, they may struggle to make decisions and take actions in their adult years.

There is another benefit to the risk-taking nature of young people. They learn to compare possible negative consequences against positive outcomes in a highly efficient way. Because of this efficiency in calculating risk, a younger person is more likely to take advantage of opportunities that may feel risky to older generations. For example, Kickstarter is a program that allows people to invest in new ideas. The program is mostly used by young people who can raise money to start businesses, and many of these businesses offer innovative products and services. Younger people have also introduced new sports such as snowboarding, which is now an Olympic sport, and thousands have used the Internet to create their own entertainment channels. YouTube celebrities might also gain fame (and money) by eating strange food on camera or by producing hair and makeup demonstrations that attract a million viewers.

Romer does not want to minimize public concern about children. When it comes to dangers such as drinking and driving, he agrees that a certain percentage of teens go too far and continue risky behavior, particularly if they never develop impulse control. These are the teens that drive their cars into trees late at night and cause insurance rates to rise. Most teens, however, have control over their decisions and learn to balance the risks with the rewards. For example, many young people skip school once, but they do not continue the behavior because the experience teaches them that the negative consequence is greater than the reward.

Adults may not always appreciate this ability to learn from risky mistakes. Romer believes that adults think differently from teens because adults have moved through the experience-gathering stage of development. They can make judgments based on their accumulated memories, so their brains do not need risk as much. This ability to use experience is often called wisdom, and while adults wish they could just transfer their own wisdom to their children, their children's biology has a different plan.

So, while teenagers will eventually develop the wisdom of experience that adults have, both Siegel and Romer agree that adults can benefit from young people's willingness to question traditional ways of thinking and behaving. Without the challenges presented by teenagers, the older generation can hold onto rigid ways of thinking. They may be less open to new ideas and even get bored or depressed. When teens challenge tradition, they open up possibilities for creative thinking that can bring hope and inspiration to a community.

Society can also support teens by providing positive environments for risk-taking. For example, speaking in front of an audience by joining a debate team or performing in a play can be scary. Also, going camping or participating in sports such as rock-climbing requires risk. And volunteering in a homeless shelter or doing other charity work can provide an opportunity for young people to test their courage and gather valuable experience.

In fact, positive risk can increase happiness. A study by Dr. Eva Telzer of the University of Illinois at Urbana-Champaign showed that teens who volunteer to help others have less depression than teens who do not. Dr. Telzer noted that the experience was particularly beneficial in the more personally risky context of helping strangers. Her findings add further support to the notion that positive risk-taking creates a win-win situation for both teens and society.

The skateboard park in Seattle is an example of this move to support the younger population. Before they had a park, skateboarders caused many accidents because they practiced in parking garages and pedestrian areas. The city finally recognized that these kids were going to take physical risks no matter what, so they created a space where that risk could be minimized. Also, if someone does get hurt, it is more likely that others will be there to help. Now there are skateboard parks in many cities, and there are fewer serious accidents.

Discussion

1. What is a risk that you took and learned from? (Or talk about someone you know.)

2. Do you know someone who missed an opportunity because they were not willing to take a risk?

3. There are several types of risks, including physical risks such as rock-climbing, financial risks such as starting a business, and social risks such as performing in a show. What type of risk do you prefer?

Insight sentences

1. This conversation made me think more about _____.

2. A scientific understanding of the teenage brain can help society because _____

_____.

Attentive Listening

Collaborating with others requires good listening skills. When people have your attention, they can talk through their ideas. When you have their attention, you can talk through yours. Then you can work together to put the best ideas into action. Good listeners remember the ideas they hear. Then they respond to those ideas before they transition to their own ideas.

Use one of the stems below to rephrase the speaker's ideas.

- I got you. You think . . .
- Uh-huh. You get a lot out of . . .
- So I think you are saying . . .
- I like your point about . . .

To transition, use one of the stems below to add or comment.

- So here's what I think:
- But don't you ever feel that . . . ?
- Yeah, you're exactly right, and I also think . . .
- What you said about . . . makes me want to learn more about . . .

ATTENTIVE LISTENING

Form groups of four or five people to practice attentive listening. Choose a risk from the list below and then have a conversation. What can the risk-taker learn? Does it have positive or negative consequences or both?

Risks

- Sneaking out of the house without your parents knowing in the middle of the night
- Climbing a tree, jumping off a bridge, or some other dangerous physical activity
- Doing something in front of an audience such as giving a speech, participating in a debate, or acting in a play
- Changing your appearance in some way such as dyeing your hair or wearing unusual clothes, make up, or jewelry
- Entering a contest or competition

Use the sentence stems from the box above and/or your own ideas.

a. Choose a timekeeper. The timekeeper sets a phone timer for three or four minutes and monitors the speakers to make sure they listen attentively. The timekeeper should also make sure everyone has a chance to speak at least once before time runs out.

b. The first speaker chooses a topic and starts the conversation. Next, group members respond by restating the speaker's main ideas before sharing their opinions and experiences.

c. No group member may speak again until every other person in the group has spoken.

d. At the end of the time, everyone discusses the experience and how they felt.

Rising Water

READ THE SCRIPT

 Read *Rising Water*. Make notes. Then discuss the questions that follow.

THE PLAY takes place in a coastal city on the Atlantic Ocean or the Gulf of Mexico. It is the near future, and society is beginning to experience changing weather patterns.

Settings: The Cooper household, a restaurant, city streets, and a downtown public library.

At times, the stage is divided into two areas. The Cooper home is always stage left, and the library scenes are always stage right. Other scenes can be center stage.

CAST

Ajax Cooper: (late teens) a high school teenager (If played by a female, her name is Jane.)

Magnus Horst: (late teens) Ajax's neighbor and classmate (If played by a female, her name is Margaret.)

Ivy Cooper: (15) Ajax's younger sister (If played by a male, his name is Trey.)

Sara Cooper: (mid-40s) Ajax's mother

Gordon Cooper: (late 40s) Ajax's father

Petra Lewis: (30s) restaurant owner (If played by a male, his name is Peter)

Mrs. Peele: (late 20s/early 30s) librarian (If played by a male, his name is Mr. Peele)

Note: The roles of Petra and Ivy can be played by the same actress if necessary because they are not in the same scenes.

Scene 1: *A bus stop in the rain. Ajax is pacing up and down the stage. Magnus sits and watches.*

Ajax: (*Looks at his phone or watch*) I'm in trouble.

Magnus: Yes you are!

Ajax: (*Sarcastically*) That's helpful, Magnus.

Magnus: I'm just sayin'. Your interview is at 3, right?

Ajax: Yes, and it's not my fault. It's the bus.

Magnus: (*Looks at his phone*) It's late.

Ajax: I know it's late. But when is it going to get here?

Magnus: It's raining. The bus is always slow when it rains.

Ajax: I should have left sooner.

Magnus: If you had studied for the test, you could have finished in time. You probably just missed the 2:10.

Ajax: Well, why aren't you on the 2:10?

Magnus: Because I was talking to my teacher about an extra credit project. I don't have a job interview, so I didn't need to leave early.

Ajax: Yeah . . . well . . .

Magnus: It's all about planning ahead, Ajax.

Ajax: Yeah well, I'm not you, Magnus. You're perfect. Everyone knows that.

Magnus: I'm not perfect, Ajax. I'm organized. I plan ahead.

Ajax: Can we talk about something else?

Magnus: Like what?

Ajax: Like . . . Where is that bus?

Magnus: Maybe it's stuck in the rain. The streets downtown flood, you know.

Ajax: I know.

Magnus: (*Looks at his phone again*) It's at 34th and Willow.

Ajax: (*Looks at his phone or watch*) I've got 20 minutes to get there.

Magnus: Do you want to hear what we talked about?

Ajax: Huh?

Magnus: With my teacher. We talked about CRISPR (*pronounced "crisper"*).

Ajax: What's CRISPR?

Magnus: It's gene editing. When we have children, we'll be able to pick out their characteristics.

Ajax: Like what? Like a boy or a girl?

Magnus: Mm-hmm. You can choose gender, hair color, intelligence, lots of things.

Ajax: Yeah?

Magnus: Yeah.

Ajax: And you think that's a good thing?

Magnus: It's not good or bad; it's just how it'll be.

Ajax: Then all the kids will be like you, Magnus.

Magnus: You think?

Ajax: Yes, the world will be full of brainy kids. They'll always be on time and they'll read science books on Saturday.

Magnus: (*A little smug*) Well, society does need people who can solve the problems of the 21st century.

Ajax: (*Sighs loudly*) I don't get you.

Magnus: What?

Ajax: Ordering your kid from a lab? It's like creating a robot.

Magnus: Oh, I wouldn't say that.

Ajax: There will be tons of kids like you—nice, safe kids with big brains.

Magnus: (*Frowns*) I don't know. . .

Ajax: That's going to be so boring.

Magnus: No! Not necessarily.

Ajax: Well, you're the model child, Magnus, so you're alright, aren't you? People like me will disappear.

Magnus: What do you mean?

Ajax: Oh yeah, I can see it now. I want a kid who doesn't do his homework. And, like, he doesn't clean his room, that's going to be great. Really, Magnus, do you think my parents would have chosen my genes?

Magnus: Uh, I'd rather not answer that.

Ajax: Yeah, well I guess I'm lucky I live now! Cause if I lived in the future, I'd never be born.

Magnus: Huh? If you lived in the future, you'd never be born? That doesn't make any sense.

Ajax: You know what I mean.

Magnus: Look at this way. You'd never know anyway because you wouldn't exist!

Ajax: (*Sarcastically*) Yeah, well that makes me feel good.

Magnus: (*Raises hands in a gesture of acceptance*) Okay, Okay. I get it. (*Pause*) Anyway, some parents might like a kid that's, you know, challenging.

Ajax: (*Shrugs*) I see it! There's the bus! Finally!

(*Both stand and put up their hoods or hold books or something over their heads as if standing in the rain as they wait for the bus.*)

Scene 2: *The Cooper household. Sara Cooper is standing and watching the news on the television or even on a laptop. She has a spatula or wooden spoon in her hand as if she has been interrupted from her cooking. She hears a noise and turns her head toward the "door." Gordon enters wearing a raincoat or maybe with an umbrella.*

Gordon: I'm home!

Sara: (*Turns off the television*) What a relief! How is it out there?

Gordon: Pretty bad.

Sara: Did you have any trouble? Car okay?

Gordon: It wasn't great, but I'm glad I left early. (*He takes off his raincoat.*) I took Willow Street.

Sara: Good idea. Main always floods.

Gordon: That's what I was thinking. Willow had some water though. And everyone was leaving at the same time.

Sara: I know. I went to the store, and I couldn't get to the parking lot.

Gordon: Really?

Sara: Yeah. I needed chicken. I'm making soup for Ivy.

Gordon: Good. How is she? Is she still sick?

Sara: Uh-huh. She hasn't eaten anything all day.

Gordon: (*Sighs*) Right. So, is she still in bed?

Sara: Yes. She's sleeping.

Gordon: I hear the flu is going around. Do you think she has the flu?

Sara: I hope not. It's really bad this year. A lot of people are in the hospital!

Gordon: Well, rest and sleep, right? What about Ajax? Is he here?

Sarah: No.

Gordon: (*Alarmed*) Where is he?

Sara: (*A little frustrated*) I don't know. Downtown, I think. He has a job interview, remember?

Gordon: That's not good. He's going to get stuck. Have you talked to him?

Sara: (*Gestures with palms up in frustration.*) No. I called and texted. No answer.

Gordon: That is so like Ajax!

Sara: I know.

Gordon: This is not acceptable Sara. We need to be able to reach him.

Sara: I know. I know. I did reach Magnus, and he said Ajax was on the 72 bus.

Gordon: (*Goes to the window and pretends to push back a curtain*) Where is it?

Sara: Where is what? The bus? How would I know?

Gordon: No, not the bus. The interview.

Sara: Oh, a restaurant downtown. One of those places around the fountain. I thought I told you.

Gordon: Yeah, but do you know which restaurant?

Sara: Something that starts with P. Patty's, maybe. I don't remember.

Gordon: And Magnus doesn't know?

Sara: No, I asked.

Gordon: Where is Magnus now?

Sara: At the library. He says he's going to stay there until the rain stops.

Gordon: Did he say where Ajax got off?

Sara: I suppose it would be near the fountain.

Gordon: Let's try again. (*Gordon takes out his phone and makes the call. Sara goes to the window and looks out. She shakes her head.*)

Sara: It's getting worse.

Gordon: (*Into the phone*) Hey, Ajax, I'm hoping you pick up. Your mother and I are worried about you. Can you call as soon as you get this message?

Sara: I can't see the street!

(*Gordon goes over to the window and looks out.*)

Gordon: Wow! I've never seen it like that!

Sara: I know! I wish Ajax would call!

Gordon: He's not thinking! You'd think he'd at least let us know where he is.

Sara: Yeah, yeah. I know. He's probably stuck somewhere. Maybe his phone got wet.

Gordon: That's a new phone! It had better not be wet.

Sara: Let's look at the bright side. He *is* getting a job.

Gordon: Yes, but he's making some poor decisions along the way. Who goes to a job interview in the middle of a flood?

Sara: He wants to make a good impression!

Gordon: Let me try again. (*He makes another call.*)

Sara: Gordon, I think he'd call if he could.

Gordon: (*Into the phone*) Ajax, it's me again. If we don't hear from you, I'm going to have to come out there and look for you. I'd rather not, but I will. (*He hangs up.*)

Sara: (*Clicks on the television again*) Look. They are saying people shouldn't go out.

Gordon: So, if I am going, I need to go now.

Sara: You just got home! Are you sure?

Gordon: Well, it's not going to get any easier. Are you and Ivy going to be okay?

Sara: I guess so. But . . .

Gordon: Okay, I'm going. I'm going to drive to the bridge and walk from there. He's going to one of those restaurants around the fountain. Is that right?

Sara: That's what Magnus said.

Gordon: I'll just go there and call when I find him. I promise.

Sara: Okay then. You want a plastic bag for your phone? So it doesn't get wet?

Gordon: Yeah. (*Sara hands him a sandwich bag*)

Sara: And you promise to stay in contact?

Gordon: Right. I promise.

(*Sara and Gordon exit. The stage is bare for a moment. Then Ajax walks across the stage lifting his feet high and his arms up as though walking through high water.*)

Scene 3: *A downtown restaurant. The owner, Petra, is doing some paperwork. Ajax walks in.*

Petra: We're closed.

Ajax: Oh, I'm sorry. I'm not a customer. I'm here for a job interview. My name is Ajax. Ajax Cooper.

Petra: Hi, Ajax. Weren't you supposed to be here 30 minutes ago?

Ajax: Yes, but the rain . . . Um. . . The bus was late.

Petra: (*Understanding*) Yeah, I get it, not your fault. Look, um, I'm sorry, but it looks pretty bad out there. I got a weather alert a couple of minutes ago, so I think we may have to put this off for another day.

Ajax: Okay. I'll just go then. (*He hesitates.*)

Petra: I'm really sorry you came all this way, but if it helps, I'm impressed you made it!

Ajax: Oh, um, thanks, I guess. (*He nods*) I totally understand. I probably should have called, but I forgot my phone on the bus. (*He turns around to leave.*)

Petra: Ajax, wait!

(*Ajax turns*)

Petra: Do you have a ride? How are you going to get home?

Ajax: The bus.

Petra: Are you sure?

Ajax: Yeah, I'll be fine.

Petra: Where do you live?

Ajax: The north side.

Petra: Oh! The water is rising over there.

Ajax: I'll be fine.

Petra: (*Looks at her phone.*) The freeway is flooded. The buses aren't going to be running.

Ajax: They're not? Are you sure?

Petra: No. Is there somewhere else you can go?

Ajax: Oh yeah. I'll figure it out.

Petra: (*Doubtful*) I kind of feel responsible here. What are you going to do?

Ajax: My friend is at the library. I'll go there.

Petra: (*Relieved*) Oh, are you sure? Because if you can't get there, I guess you could. . .

Ajax: No, it's fine. It's really not that far.

Petra: Okay then, if you're sure.

Ajax: Yeah. My friend's always trying to get me to go to the library, so now I'm going!

Petra: Do you want to call him?

Ajax: I don't know his number.

Petra: Yeah, phones, right? How about your family? You said you don't have your phone with you.

Ajax: Um, no I don't. I don't remember their numbers either.

Petra: Really?

Ajax: It's okay. If I can get to my friend, he can connect us.

Petra: Right. So, you have a plan. That's good then. (*She turns back to her paperwork.*)

Ajax: Yes, um, should I call you later? To reschedule?

Petra: (*Looks up.*) Yes, next week. This flood is going to be a disaster. We'll probably have to close for a few days.

Ajax: Okay, I'll be in touch. Bye.

Petra: Bye! Stay safe!

(*Ajax leaves. Petra looks out the window and shakes her head. Lights out.*)

Scene 4: *The street, Ivy's bedroom, and an upstairs area of the public library.*

The stage is empty. Gordon walks across the stage as if wading through deep water. He is holding his shoes over his head in one hand. He has a phone in a plastic bag in his other hand, also held over his head. He crosses the stage, nearly loses his balance, and then recovers. Then he comes back. He looks around. Then he goes upstage center and stands still, holding his shoes and phone above his waist. He looks out as if at the water.

Sara and Ivy enter. Ivy lies on the floor or a table. Sarah sits next to her with a bowl of soup. (stage left)

Ivy: I don't want any soup.

Sara: You have to eat something! You haven't eaten for three days.

Ivy: Mom, I'm not hungry. I'm sick.

Sara: Just a little soup. One bite.

Ivy: It's just going to make it worse.

Sara: You're so hot!

(*Ivy sighs.*)

Sara: I made this especially for you! It's just a little chicken and vegetables. You need fluids.

Ivy: I don't want it.

Sara: Come on, just try one bite. You want to get better, don't you?

Ivy: The smell is making me sick.

Sara: How about some water then?

Ivy: I don't want any water. I'm tired.

Sara: Let me take your temperature.

Ivy: Why? I already know I have a fever.

Sara: (*Takes a thermometer and puts it under Ivy's tongue.*) Just let me see. Hold still. Your dad is out looking for Ajax. No, don't try to say anything. Just hold it. There. . . that's right. He went downtown, but all the restaurants are closed. Wouldn't you know? Now he has to get back, and the bridge is under water. Ajax still hasn't called, so everything is a huge mess! I don't know what to do!

(*Pause. She takes out the thermometer and looks it. She looks again and is alarmed.*) Ivy, your temperature! I'm calling a doctor.

Ivy: Just let me sleep, Mom.

Sara: Okay, okay, but can you please try to drink this, just a little? You'll get dehydrated.

Ivy: I'm not thirsty. I don't want it.

Sara: Please? For me?

(*Ivy tries to sit up. Sara helps her and gives her some soup from a cup. Ivy drinks and coughs. Then falls back on the bed.*)

Ivy: There. That's enough.

(*Gordon takes out his phone and makes a call. He looks out over the audience as he speaks. Sara stands and also turns to face the audience as she answers it.*)

Sara: Hello. Gordon?

Gordon: Have you heard from Ajax?

Sara: (*Worried*) No! What about you? Where are you?

Gordon: I'm near the train station. But the water is getting higher. I've never seen it like this! It's up to my waist!

Sara: Are you going to be okay?

Gordon: Yes.

Sara: Wait, Gordon. I'm going to put you on hold. There's a call from Magnus. Hang on.

(*Ajax walks on stage right. He's holding a phone. He also looks out over the audience as he talks. Gordon looks away from the audience.*)

Sara: Magnus?

Ajax: Hi, Mom. It's me, Ajax.

Sara: Oh, Thank God! Are you okay?

Ajax: Yes, I'm fine, Mom. I didn't get to do the interview.

Sara: The interview? Who cares about the interview! I just want to know that you're okay. Your father is looking for you!

Ajax: Oh, he didn't need to do that. I'm okay.

Sara: Well, we didn't know that, did we? You didn't answer our calls, our texts. What were we supposed to think?

Ajax: Um, yeah, about that . . . I left my phone on the bus.

Sara: Oh, Ajax (*Worried*). Your father is at the train station.

Ajax: Uh oh.

Sara: What do you mean, "Uh oh."?

Ajax: I can see that part of the city from here. It's underwater.

Sara: He's on the phone right now. On hold.

Ajax: Tell him to leave. See if he can get here to the library. It's staying open.

Sara: Don't hang up. (*She transfers to Gordon. Gordon looks up, and Ajax turns away.*)

Sara: Gordon, Ajax is okay. He's at the library. He says it's safe there. Can you get to the library?

Gordon: The water's pretty high. I might have to swim. (*He laughs*)

Sara: You don't know how to swim, Gordon! I told you to take lessons.

Gordon: Well, it's a little late now!

Ivy: Mom? I feel bad. I'm so hot!

Sara: (*to Ivy*) Shh, sweetheart. I'm talking to your father.

Gordon: Okay, so I'll try to get there, and I might lose the signal. But don't worry. I'll be careful.

Sara: Magnus has a phone. Look for Magnus and call me as soon as you get there.

Gordon: I will.

Sara: (*Transfers call. Gordon looks away and Ajax looks up and at the audience again.*) Ajax? Your father's going to try to get to you. Stay there. Do NOT leave.

Ajax: Mom . . .

Ivy: Mom. . . I'm hot. I'm so hot.

Sara: (*Looks at Ivy*) I gotta go, Ajax. Just. Stay. Safe! You hear me?

(*Lights out*)

Scene 5: *Flood waters outside the train station.*

Gordon walks onto the stage again. His hands holding his shoes are even higher. He gets halfway across the stage. He looks to the left and the right. The water is too high. He goes back. Suddenly, Ajax appears with a life jacket or other flotation device. He mimes swimming.

Ajax: Dad!

Gordon: Ajax! What are you doing here? You're supposed to be at the library.

Ajax: Yeah, Dad, can we talk about that later? You need to get out of here.

Gordon: I can't. I'm stuck. I can't swim.

Ajax: I know, Dad. That's why I'm here. Take this. Hold on and don't let go!

Gordon: What about the phone? It'll get wet.

Ajax: Who cares about the phone? You can get another one.

Gordon: I need this phone!

Ajax: Dad!

Gordon: I don't know about this.

Ajax: You don't have a choice! (*Pause*) Okay, Give me the phone. And just grab onto this.

(*Gordon passes the phone to Ajax, who holds it up. Gordon puts on the life jacket or takes the flotation device. Gordon hesitates.*)

Gordon: I can't.

Ajax: Trust me.

(Ajax mimes leading Gordon into the water.)

(Lights out)

Scene 6 *Ivy's Bedroom, stage left. The library, stage right.*

Magnus is in the library (stage right), sitting down and reading a book. He is not aware of Gordon and Ajax as they walk in with Mrs. Peele. They have blankets around them if possible. The blankets can make it look as if they have come in out of the rain. Also, they can push their hands over their heads as if trying to get wet hair out of their faces.

Mrs. Peele: (*Talking nervously*) I don't know how you two got here! The water at the train station must have been over your heads! I've never seen anything like this!

Gordon: It was. (*Looks at Ajax.*) My son here rescued me.

Mrs. Peele: Wow! And just in time. You really shouldn't be out in that water, either of you! You both need to stay here until the rain stops.

Gordon: I think we have to. I'm so sorry. We don't want to make trouble.

Mrs. Peele: No, don't worry about it. It's no trouble at all. We've got the doors open for anyone who is stranded. Lucky thing the library is on high ground. I'm stuck, too! But I'm lucky. My family is fine. They're all over on the East Side.

Gordon: That must be a relief.

Mrs. Peele: It is. And what about your family?

Gordon: (*Looks at Ajax*) Well, they're north. I think they are okay, but my daughter is sick, so I'd like to check in.

Mrs. Peele: Of course. Of course.

Ajax: We can use my friend's phone. Thank you, Mrs. Peele. He's over there.

Mrs. Peele: Oh good.

Gordon: I see him! (*Turns to Mrs. Peele*) We really appreciate this.

Mrs. Peele: Oh, don't worry. At times like this, we all take care of each other.

Ajax: Exactly. I want to help. Who should I talk to?

Mrs. Peele: We are okay for now. You just stay here until the rain stops. That's what they say on the news: Stay where you are.

Gordon: Yes, we will. Ajax, come on. We need to call your mother.

(*Gordon and Ajax walk over to Magnus. Magnus looks up with relief.*)

Magnus: You're okay!

Ajax: Yeah, we made it.

Gordon: You okay? Is your family okay?

Magnus: Oh yeah, they're high and dry. But I'm a little worried about your house.

Ajax: Have you talked to my mom?

Magnus: Not much. I'm trying to save my battery. You can call her now. (*Magnus dials and hands the phone to Gordon. The phone rings several times. Then Ivy crawls on stage from the left side and picks it up.*)

Ivy: (*Weakly*) Hello?

Gordon: Sara?

Ivy: Dad?

Gordon: Ivy? It's you. Are you okay?

Ivy: I'm sick! I thought you were mom.

Gordon: Ivy, is your mother there?

Ivy: I don't know.

Gordon: Ivy, talk to me. What's going on? Where is she?

Ivy: Dad, I'm really sick.

Gordon: Did she leave you?

Ivy: Maybe. . . She said something about medicine. I gotta go, Dad. I can't talk. I'm tired.

Gordon: Tell her we're safe. Tell her we're at the library.

Ivy: Library . . . we're at the library.

Gordon: Ivy?

(*Ivy lies back down. Sara comes in stage left.*)

Sara: Who was that?

Ivy: Dad.

Sara: Where is he?

Ivy: I don't know.

Sara: Did you tell him the electricity is out?

Ivy: I don't feel good.

Sara: Ivy, we need to get out of here. They're evacuating the neighborhood. They say we have to go.

Ivy: I can't move.

Sara: Okay, so let me think. (*Pause*) Maybe I can get you upstairs. Can you walk?

Ivy: No. . .

Sara: Just lean on me.

(*Sara puts her arm around Ivy and helps her offstage.*)

(*Lights out*)

Scene 7 *The library. Gordon and Magnus are sitting. Ajax is walking up and down impatiently.*

Gordon: We need to get back home.

(*Mrs. Peele appears with some food.*)

Mrs. Peele: You can't go home. The streets are closed. The freeway is a river. There's no way.

Gordon: My wife and daughter are still in our house.

Mrs. Peele: We can call emergency response. They'll send someone. Give me the address. There's a dispatch operator downstairs. Write it down, here and I'll get it to her. It's the fastest way. (*Mrs. Peele gives Gordon some paper and a pen. Gordon writes his address and hands it to her. She puts it in her pocket absent-mindedly. Ajax starts to say something. He gestures to her pocket, but he is interrupted by Magnus.*)

Magnus: I just got a text. Mrs. Cooper and Ivy are upstairs. They say the downstairs is flooded.

Ajax: I'm going there, Dad.

Gordon: No, you're not!

Ajax: Dad, I have to. I can't stay here. I have to do something.

Gordon: You'll just make things worse.

Mrs. Peele: Your father's right, Ajax. The rescue teams have enough to worry about. If you get into trouble out there, you'll just make more work for them.

Gordon: She's right. You'll put them in danger trying to rescue you. Then they won't be able to help other victims. You don't want that, do you?

Ajax: Dad, that's not going to happen!

Gordon: You'll help the most if you just stay here where you're safe.

Ajax: You didn't stay safe. You came out.

Gordon: That's different.

Ajax: No it's not.

Gordon: Ajax. Try to understand.

Ajax: I don't want to be safe! I want to go out and help!

Gordon: I know you do. But we have to let the authorities handle it. They know what they're doing.

Ajax: So do I. I helped you!

Gordon: I know, and that was too risky. You were lucky.

Mrs. Peele: Your family is going to be fine, Ajax. Emergency crews are trained for this, and we'll get your family on their list. It's the safest way.

Magnus: They've got a point, Ajax!

(*Ajax continues walking up and down. He looks out the "window" over the audience's heads.*)

Ajax: Look, there are boats out there!

Mrs. Peele: Yes, exactly! The authorities are taking care of the situation.

Ajax: (*Looks closely*) Yeah, well I see regular people, too. There's a couple of guys out there with plastic garbage backs over their clothes. It's not just authorities. See?

Gordon: (*Doesn't go over to Ajax.*) How about we talk about something else? We can play a game or something.

Ajax: I don't want to play a game. How can you just sit here and do nothing?

Mrs. Peele and **Gordon** together: It's too dangerous!

Ajax: (*Sighs impatiently and looks at them.*) Okay, fine!

(*Pause*)

I'm thirsty; I'm going to go get some water. Anyone want anything? (*He starts to back away.*)

Mrs. Peele: I think we have some games here. Would you like to look?

Gordon: (*to Mrs. Peele*) Okay.

(Mrs. Peele and Gordon move downstage and look silently at an imaginary shelf. They are facing away from Magnus and Ajax.)

Magnus: *(to Ajax)* I'll go with you.

Ajax: No, that's okay; I'll get you some. You stay here in case my mom calls. Be back in a second.

Magnus: Ajax?

Ajax: What?

Magnus: *(Realizes that Ajax is going to leave.)* Are you sure you don't want me to go with you?

Ajax: I'm just getting a drink of water!

Magnus: Yeah but . . . Okay, never mind.

Ajax: I gotta go. *(He leaves.)*

(Magnus sits.)

Mrs. Peele: Your son is very brave. You must be proud of him.

Gordon: I am. I wish he knew that. He's always been a difficult child, but that doesn't mean we don't care about him, you know?

Mrs. Peele: I know.

Gordon: He used to scare us to death when he was a child. He'd climb trees, fences, anything. His mother caught him on the roof and nearly had a heart attack!

Mrs. Peele: Some boys are like that.

Magnus: I'm not!

Mrs. Peele: *(Looks at him)* No, you don't seem like the adventurous type. But the world needs all kinds of people, don't you think? Some like books. I think that's you and me. Others just need adventure.

Gordon: *(turns around and looks for Ajax)* Where's Ajax?

Magnus: He said he was thirsty.

Gordon: Uh oh.

Magnus: Ummmm. Yeah, he said he was going to get some water.

Gordon: I think I better check, just to make sure. I love Ajax, but I don't trust him.

(*Petra appears with a blanket around her shoulders.*)

Gordon: Oh, hello. I didn't see you. Are you okay?

Petra: No, not really.

Gordon: Uh okay. What do you need?

Petra: I need a drink! I'm soaking wet, and my restaurant is ruined.

Gordon: I'm so sorry. (*Gordon turns to Mrs. Peele*) Can you help her?

Petra: This is the worst day of my life!

Mrs. Peele: I'm sure it is, but we'll get through it.

(*Mrs. Peele brings Petra over to a chair.*)

Magnus: Um, Mrs. Peele, what about the address? Do you want me to call the emergency response?

Gordon: (*Alarmed*) We haven't done that yet?

Mrs. Peele: (*Confused for a moment*) Oh, right. I forgot. Yes, just a second. (*Turns to Petra.*) Are you going to be okay?

Gordon: Don't bother. I'll go tell them. It's my family and I've got to find Ajax anyway. (*He turns and starts walking offstage*) Ajax! Ajax? Ajax?

Magnus: He's not going to find him.

Mrs. Peele: What do you mean?

Magnus: Ajax isn't getting water to drink, Mrs. Peele; he's out in the flood. I'll bet you one hundred dollars he's left the building. He's probably out on one of those boats right now.

Mrs. Peele: Why didn't you say something? We can't let him go out there.

Magnus: Well, it's too late now. I'm pretty sure he's out on a boat by now.

Petra: Who is Ajax?

(*Lights out*)

Scene 8: *Upstairs in the Cooper home. Sara and Ivy are in the attic now. Sara bends over Ivy.*

Sara: Ivy, stay with me.

Ivy: (*Weakly*) Where am I?

Sara: You're in the attic, dear.

Ivy: I'm late for school, Mom. I've got to get up.

Sara: You're not going to school, Ivy. You're sick.

Ivy: (*Confused*) But I have to go to school.

Sara: Shh. Be still, Ivy. Everything is going to be okay. Try to rest. Oh gosh. You're too hot!

Ivy: But my speech. I have to give a speech. Mrs. Feldman said . . .

Sara: No you don't. . . Shh. It's okay. Help is coming.

Ivy: Okay, good night, mom! (*Ivy loses consciousness.*)

Sara: (*Looks at her phone.*) Oh no! 10 percent! (*She starts a call.*) Hello? Yes, I need help. I'm with my daughter. We are upstairs, 312 Maple, and we're trapped. We can't get out. My daughter is very sick. She needs medical attention. . . Yes. We need help, now! . . . No, I can't stay on the line. My battery is dying. This is my last call . . . Hello? Hello? (*She looks at her phone and throws it down angrily.*) Useless!

(*Sara picks up Ivy's hand and pushes her hair off her face. There is silence for a few seconds, then Ajax calls from offstage.*)

Ajax: Mom!

Sara: Ajax?

Ajax: (*Enters*) I'm here, mom. I found some volunteers. We've got a boat. We'll get you out of here! It's going to be okay.

[*Curtain*]

DISCUSS THE PLAY

Talk about the play in groups. Share your thoughts with the class.

1. How do Magnus and Ajax represent different types of teenagers?

2. Ajax starts out feeling inferior and Magnus starts out feeling superior. How does this change during the play?

3. What mistakes do the adults in the play make? Why do they make them?

4. What kind of a person is Petra? How do you know?

5. What kind of person is Mrs. Peele? How do you know?

6. What is the message of the play? (What does it say about teenagers, risk-taking, and/or the future?)

Production

Perform your play for your class or another class. You may also choose to video your play. Here are some suggestions for rehearsing and performing.

a. **Rehearsed reading** (also called Reader's Theater): Actors work with a director and the script. They sit or stand in one place. A stage manager reads the scene information at the beginning and end of a scene. Then the actors read the parts with a focus on emotion, stress, and intonation. (When actors are not in a scene it can be helpful to have them turn their backs to the audience.)

b. **Staged reading** (another form of Reader's Theater): Actors work with a director and the script. They also block the play. This means they move around the stage and work with props and a set just like in a theatrical production. However, they carry and read from a script when they need to.

c. **Full performance:** Actors prepare their roles, memorize their lines, and block the play. They perform for an audience just like in a real theatre.

d. **Video:** Work with a videographer to record the performance. Find a quiet place to film so the microphone does not pick up extra noise. Also make sure the actors speak loudly and clearly. Edit the film and watch it later with your teacher, your group, or the whole class.

For resources on ways to perform the play, go to http://www.alphabetpublishingbooks.com/integrated-skills-through-drama/.

ANALYZE THE PLAY

Reread the play silently. Answer the questions on the following page by taking a few notes on your own. Then discuss your answers in a group.

The Story	*Notes*
The main characters of a story usually face challenges. They need to take action, but things get in their way. These obstacles can come from their own fear, other people, physical obstacles, or even nature. What personal challenges do the characters face in *Rising Water*?	
A social issue is something that citizens of a community are discussing. They want to make good decisions about how to make life better for society. In your opinion, what social issues are raised in *Rising Water*? (There can be more than one!)	
A play should have a personal connection. The audience should empathize with one or more characters. Do you feel similar to any of the people in *Rising Water*? Explain. Do you know people who have similar challenges to the people in *Rising Water*?	

ASSIGN ROLES

Decide who will play which character. There are different ways to do this.

- Give the director/teacher the names of two or three characters you are willing to play. Then that person assigns roles.
- Audition for a part. Read one scene with another student as one or more characters. The director/teacher assigns roles.
- Form groups and work together to decide who will play which part.

LEARN YOUR PART

Read the play again and highlight your lines in yellow. Then make decisions about your character's personality and emotions. The following activities can help.

a. Read the vocabulary describing emotional states and the first example. Write a second example from your own experience or the play. Which words describe your character?

	Example one	*Example two*
accommodating	Chris does not eat meat, but she cooks meat dishes for her family.	
agitated	Kiki is biting her nails and walking up and down while she waits for the doctor to tell her whether she is sick or not.	
brainy	Raul takes the highest-level math and physics classes. He plans on becoming a rocket scientist.	
self-pitying	Ed tells his friends he has a terrible life because he has to use an old phone.	
ill at ease	Sven is not good at starting conversations, so he feels uncomfortable at parties.	
impulsive	Terry decides to climb a tree without thinking about how she will get back down.	
inferior	Tia was not invited to join the sports team. She's hurt, and it is hard for her to listen to others talking about it.	
rebellious	Neda disobeys her parents and does not go to her Saturday math class. Instead she goes shopping with friends.	

reckless	Li rides his motorcycle fast and does not wear a helmet.	
relieved	Wes's two-year-old daughter gets lost in a store. When Wes finds her, he is very happy she is safe.	
reluctant	Dill wants to take the bus because he doesn't trust my driving. I argue that the bus will take too long, so he has agreed to go in my car if I promise to be careful.	
sarcastic	Rex says, "Good job!" when Sam forgets to bring the paperwork to the meeting.	
superior	Jen feels he should always sit in the front seat of the car because he is better than others.	

b. Practice getting comfortable expressing feelings and intentions.

c. Develop your character. Decide how your character feels in different scenes. Use the emotion vocabulary or your ideas to make notes on your script, just as you did in the game above. Also think about why you have that feeling.

d. Memorize your lines. Choose from the following strategies. It will take several rehearsals to remember everything. Overlearn your part so you do not forget later.

* Read your part out loud two or three times a day. Read in different locations such as a coffee shop, in the park, or on the bus.
* Record yourself saying the lines. Listen to the recording and try to improve your pronunciation, speed, and volume. You'll need to speak loudly and clearly in performance.
* Read while standing. Think about your movements and your tone of voice.
* Read with a friend who can say the other characters' lines.

PLAY ON EMOTIONS

Develop your acting and communication skills through this simple game.

Play

1. Prepare by thinking of an emotion from the box above for each of the sentences below. Write the emotion next to the sentence, but do not show it to anyone.
2. Get in groups of 4 or 5 and designate someone to be a timekeeper.
3. The timekeeper sets a clock for two minutes.
4. Speaker **A** chooses a sentence from the list and says it in a way that communicates the selected emotion. The speaker can use body language, gesture, and voice to communicate the emotion, but may not say the emotion. He or she may read the sentence more than once or add details to help communicate the intended emotional state.
5. Other members of the group try to guess the emotion. The person who guesses the emotion gets a point.
6. Speaker **B** takes a turn. The game continues until all people in the group have been speaker or the time for the game is up. The winner is the person with the most points.

Sentences

Note that these sentences can communicate a variety of emotions. It's your voice and gesture that will show how you feel when you say them.

1. It's still raining. It's been raining all day.
2. He's probably in one of those boats right now.
3. Well, the thing is . . . My mother and sister are in there.
4. I can't just sit here and wait. I have to go do something.
5. Yes, the rain will stop, and then we can all go home.
6. Maybe he turned off his phone. That's possible, right?
7. I don't care. I don't care what anybody thinks. I'm going!
8. I'm sorry I bothered you.

REHEARSE

Read the play with other actors and talk about your characters' relationships.

    a. Use the sentence stems below or your own ideas to discuss your motivations with your scene partners.

In this scene,	
I feel insecure about myself, but I don't want you to know that.	I'm frustrated.
I feel superior.	I feel obligated to be polite.
I would like to make a good impression.	I feel sorry for myself.
My offer is not really sincere.	I don't really believe you.
I am starting to get agitated.	I'm ill at ease.
I'm pretending to go along with the plan.	I feel a lot of relief at this moment.

    b. Review pragmatics. After a rehearsal with the other actors, answer the questions below. Then discuss your answers with your scene partners.

        1. How do other characters respond to you? Does it feel natural?

        2. How do your pragmatics choices make the play dramatic? Try saying something with a different emotion. For example, try it with fear and then with confidence. Use different stress patterns, gesture, and voice until you feel comfortable.

        3. What phrases or expressions do characters use to signal their feelings? For example, *How can you just sit there?* is an expression people use when they think another person needs to take an action.

        4. Would you make the same language choices if you were in this situation in real life? Is there any dialog you would like to change? Work with your scene partners to make any changes to the script.

IMPROVISE A SCENE

Choose a situation for your improv from the list below or make up your own idea. Set a timer for 2 minutes and perform your improv for another group or the class.

- Magnus and Ajax are walking to school together. Magnus wants to give Ajax advice about his study habits. Ajax tries to change the subject.
- Petra tells Mrs. Peele about her restaurant and how hard she has worked to build a business. Mrs. Peele wants to be polite, but she has other things to do.
- Sara and Ivy talk about the storm. Ivy wants to know what is going on, but Sara doesn't want her to worry.
- Mrs. Peele and Gordon talk about Ajax. Gordon wants to go look for him, but Mrs. Peele thinks it's not safe.

Improv

Improv is short for improvisation, or the art of making something up on the spot without any planning in advance. During improv exercises, actors pretend to be their characters and they make up the conversations. Through improv, actors can:

- get to know their character's personality better.
- understand their character's relationships with other characters.
- be *in the moment* so the scene feels like real people talking to each other.
- discover the physical mannerisms of their character. For example, a character might bounce his knee to show nervous energy. Another might play with her glasses to show she is brainy or nervous.
- overcome stage fright and get comfortable in front of an audience.

FOCUS ON PRONUNCIATION

Practice the right stress and intonation. Also identify and practice any specific sounds that you have trouble with.

a. Try this activity to practice using and listening for emphasis. Work in pairs.
   Partner A: Say a line from the first column with a, b, **or** c emphasis.
   Partner B: Give feedback by saying the letter of the pattern you hear. Then switch.

Use Emphasis to Focus Meaning

People clarify the meaning of a statement by stressing certain words more forcefully than others. The following lines from *Rising Water* show how choice of emphasis communicates different meanings.

I want to **GO!** Meaning: I do not want to stay here any longer.

I **WANT** to go! Meaning: You think I don't want to go, but I do.

I want to go! Meaning: No one but me wants to go.

1.

Intonation pattern	Meaning
a. **I'VE** never seen it rain like that!	You have seen it, but I haven't.
b. I've **NEVER** seen it rain like that!	This is the first time I've seen rain like this.
c. I've never seen it rain like **THAT**!	I've seen heavy rain before, but this is more extreme.

2.

Intonation pattern	Meaning
a. At least **MY** life isn't boring!	Your life may have some advantages, but it is boring.
b. At least my **LIFE** isn't boring!	My work might not be exciting, but my life is.
c. At least my life isn't **BORING!**	I may have drama or challenges in my life, but that's better than having an unexciting life.

3.

Intonation pattern	Meaning
a. **HE** didn't need to do that.	It was not necessary for him to do it. Another person did it or could have done it.
b. He didn't **NEED** to do that.	Maybe he wanted to do it, but it was not required.
c. He didn't need to do **THAT**!	It was possible and maybe preferable for him to do a different thing.

4.

Intonation pattern	Meaning
a. **CAN** you get to the library?	The library is a good idea, but is it possible to get there?
b. Can **YOU** get to the library?	Other people are able to go to the library, but I'm not sure about you.
c. Can you get to the **LIBRARY**?	I know you can make it to the park, but the library will be harder.

b. Go back to your script, and mark nouns, verbs, adjectives, and adverbs that you want to stress. Pay careful attention to places where intonation patterns signal meaning and attitude. Try different possibilities and discuss with your scene partners.

c. Check your script for places where you ask questions. Choose the intonation pattern that will best communicate your emotion.

d. Use a recording device such as your phone to record yourself saying the lines out loud. Listen and make adjustments to stress and intonation.

e. Practice saying your lines with the other actors in the play. Help each other with intonation, pronunciation, and stress. Speak loudly and clearly.

Use Question Intonation

We usually think of questions as a way to get information. In real-life conversations, however, questions can have different meanings. Sometimes people use questions when they expect another person to agree with them. This makes speakers feel closer to each other because they share an understanding. On the other hand, people may also use questions to express doubt or even sarcasm. For this reason, intonation patterns are important because they reveal the speakers' purpose in asking a question. Here are some examples of lines from *Rising Water*.

Questions that start with a **WH** word genverally have a falling intonation.

- Where were you?

- What do you mean, "Uh oh"?

- Why aren't you on the 2:10?

Yes/no questions have a rising intonation.

- Are you okay?

- Have you heard from Ajax?

- Is there somewhere else you can go?

Tag questions usually have an up pitch. The pitch is higher when we are asking for confirmation, but the pitch goes down slightly when we are being critical or sarcastic.

- Your interview is at three, right? (request for confirmation)

- The world needs all kinds of people, don't you think? (expecting confirmation)

- Well, we didn't know that, did we? (sarcasm)

- You're alright, aren't you! I'm the one who will disappear. (hurt)

People may also repeat a statement with question intonation or use a negative question. The pitch tends to go higher for inquiry and lower for expressing doubt, disagreement, or a confirmation, but it can change depending on the speaker's emotional state and purpose.

- And you think that's a good thing? (disagreement)

- And you promise to stay in contact? (expecting confirmation)

BLOCK THE PLAY

Decide where you will stand and how you will move during the play. Practice several times. When you practice a lot, you will make fewer mistakes, and you will be less likely to laugh during your performance.

Blocking A Play

When a director and actors prepare for a performance, they plan where the cast will stand, sit, and when and how they will move. Here are some basic guidelines that can help you create a successful performance.

- All actors should avoid speaking with their backs to the audience. (In Reader's Theater, when not in a scene, actors can turn around.)
- Actors should not make eye contact with the audience. They can look over the audience's heads.
- All actors should speak loudly and clearly, not rush through their lines.
- When one actor is speaking, all other actors should look at the speaker. They should not move or attract attention in any way.
- A seated actor looking up is less powerful than a standing actor looking down.
- Actors should behave as if the story is happening to them for the first time and they are in a real conversation. Good acting is not reciting memorized lines. It is about listening and reacting to other actors with interest and emotion.

Notes on stage directions:

- Stage right means the right side of an actor who is looking at the audience. Stage left means the left side of the actor who is looking at the audience. Front and back also describe directions from the actor's position. Downstage is close to the audience. Upstage is away from the audience.
- To show a scene change, it is helpful to have someone turn off the lights for a few seconds.

    f. Work with your director to try out different ways to tell the story through gesture and the way you move your body. On the following page are some ways actors communicate emotions. Try acting them out. What emotion does each of the following gestures communicate?

- Fold your arms across your chest
- Put your hands on your hips
- Hold your hands over your head, palms outward
- Sit and look up at a speaker
- Stand and look down at a speaker
- Play with a phone or look away from the speaker
- Stand with a straight back
- Stand with a bent back
- Walk up and down the stage

- Put your hands over your eyes or in your hair
- Cover your mouth
- Put your hand over your heart
- Bow your head
- Tilt your head to the side
- Shake your head
- Roll your eyes
- Sigh loudly
- Bite your lip
- Make your hands into claws
- Look at someone's feet then their face

g. Rehearse the play with body language and movement several times. When you practice a lot, you will make fewer mistakes.

Note: When you are rehearsing or performing, a stage manager can sit next to the stage and read the script silently while you perform. Then they can read you a line if you forget.

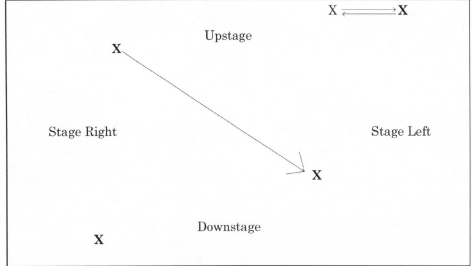

Post-Performance

 The following activities can be used to explore themes and language after a production.

LEAD A TALKBACK

The director/teacher leads the class in a conversation about the play between the actors and the audience. While there are many ways to do this, the following process can help you insure a productive discussion.

a. There is a five-minute break after the play ends while audience members take a few minutes to write some questions. Here are some examples:

  - How did you prepare for your role?
  - What decisions did your character make? Do you agree with those decisions?
  - How is your own attitude toward danger similar to or different from your character's?
  - What is the play's message?
  - Do you think it shows the truth about people?
  - Which type of teenager gets more praise in society today, kids like Magnus or kids like Ajax? Why?
  - Magnus and Ajax discuss a future in which parents can select characteristics. Ajax thinks parents will select intelligence. Do you agree?
  - What will Ajax and Magnus's life be like in other ways?

b. The director and actors come out on stage and face the audience. The director invites questions and comments. The audience asks about the play or the characters. People can direct their questions to individual actors. They can also tell how the play made them feel or what it made them think about.

WRITE AN ALTERNATIVE ENDING

Break up into groups and discuss other possible endings. Answer the questions. Then write your own scene(s).

    a. What happens in the new ending?

    b. Why does it happen?

    c. How will it affect the lives of the different people involved?

    d. Which is a better ending for the characters?

Perform your new ending for another group. Which ending is more believable and why?

GATHER LANGUAGE

Go through the script one more time. Circle phrases and stems that you want to remember for when you have important conversations. It can be helpful to look for language that helps you perform the functions below:

- Responding to criticism
- Hiding hurt feelings
- Complaining about someone
- Offering to help, accepting and declining help
- Expressing distress
- Expressing relief
- Arguing for a specific action

Note: Pay attention to how language used in casual situations is different from more formal situations.

Practice the language in role-plays by creating new situations for the characters at school, work, or among friends. Create different motivations for each. Here are some examples.

- Petra wants to talk to Gordon about problems with her restaurant. Gordon wants to politely leave so he can make a phone call.
- Sara is on the phone with a rescue boat. She is trying to give directions. The emergency operator cannot understand because of a bad connection.
- Gordon calls Sara at the hospital. He wants all the details. Sara does not want him to worry.
- Ajax wants Magnus to help clean people's houses after the storm. Magnus is afraid the work will be physically difficult, but he does not want to admit his fear.
- Petra complains about the city's response to the storm. Mrs. Peele disagrees. She thinks the emergency responders are doing a good job.

HAVE A MINI-DEBATE

Choose one of the topics below. Then form two teams and a panel of judges. Each team creates three or four arguments. Then each team member gets a turn to make one argument each. An opposing team member gets a chance to respond to each argument and make a counterargument. You may have three or four rounds of argument and counterargument. The judges can individually record up to five points for each argument. When the debate is over, the judges meet to add their points and declare a winner.

Debate Topics:

* High schools should train students for emergency situations.
* Governments should pass laws to encourage climate-friendly policies.
* Parents should be allowed to choose the genetic characteristics of their children.

See instructions and materials for structuring a mini-debate on the Alphabet Publishing website at http://www.alphabetpublishingbooks.com/integrated-skills-through-drama/.

CREATE A SEQUEL

Work with a partner or in small groups. What do you think Ajax and Magnus's life will be like in the future? Pick a time, such as five or ten years from now, and write a short play about their life. You may want to invent new characters.

* Some newspaper reporters interview Ajax and his family after the flood.
* Six years later, Magnus and Ajax meet in a park. They compare their lives today with their lives and personalities when they were in high school.
* Ten years later, Magnus is a father. His son is a little reckless, and Magnus does not know what to do. He tells his wife the story of Ajax and the flood, and they try to decide what to say to their son.
* Twelve years later, Ajax works for the city as a trainer in emergency management. He goes to a school to give a talk to some students about what to do in an emergency.

PRACTICE PRAGMATICS

Recognizing Sincere and Insincere Offers

In the scene between Petra and Ajax. Petra is polite, but she would rather not get involved in Ajax's problem. Handling situations like this with people you do not know well can be challenging.

1. Discuss your experience with one or both of the situations below. Tell the story and how it felt:
   * When was the last time you felt that someone's offer or invitation was not sincere?
   * Can you remember a time when you offered something, but you hoped the other person would not accept it?

2. Read the situations with offers below. Write *S* if you think the offer is sincere and *NS* if you think the offer is not sincere. Circle language that helps you decide?

a. Raul is struggling with his math homework, so his mother calls a friend who teaches math and explains the situation. The friend responds.

    i. ____ Oh Raul is so smart. I'm sure he'll figure it out on his own. If he doesn't, you can tell him to call me.

    ii. ____ Hey, I'd love to help. I'm not doing anything. Is he free right now? We can set up a face-to-face call.

b. Kiki is having lunch with a friend when she gets a text. Her boss needs her at work, but Kiki has to pick up her brother at his soccer practice. When she explains this to her friend, her friend responds.

    i. ____ I can't believe your boss expects you to just come whenever he wants you. If I were you, I'd pretend I didn't see the text. But I know you. You're going to say yes, and your brother will still need a ride, right?

    ii. ____ Wow, that's a lot for your boss to ask, but I understand how it is. I tell you what. Why don't I pick up your brother and meet you at your house later?

Responding to Offers

In a conversation between acquaintances (people who are not close friends or relatives), the desire to be polite can be powerful. People generally value cooperation and feel good when they help others. However, sometimes the social pressure to make an offer can create an awkward situation when the speaker does not really mean it. In this case the person may use their voice and language to signal reluctance. The other person usually, but not always, recognizes these signals and may politely decline the offer or accept it anyway.

Here is an example of how a sincere offer might work. Notice the conversation is short and fairly comfortable.

A has stopped by B's house.	B is kind but busy.
MOVE 1: Express a need Chat about the weather. Then bring up the problem you have. For example, you are traveling and need someone to take care of your pet.	
	Say how much you like the pet. Say you would be happy to take care of it.

MOVE 2: Check sincerity. Try to get confirmation. Tell B that you have other options. Give B a chance to introduce a reason not to do it.	
	Be firm about your offer. Start setting dates and making a plan.
Thank B and arrange a plan.	

Now look at the example of an offer that may be polite but is not sincere. There are several things to notice: The conversation takes longer as A investigates B's willingness and then hesitates. A makes a choice to decline B's offer. Both A and B make an effort to end the conversation in a friendly way.

A has stopped by B's house.	*B is busy but kind.*
MOVE 1: Express a need Chat about the weather. Then bring up the problem you have. For example, you are traveling and need someone to take care of your pet.	
	Avoid offering: Instead, express sympathy. Say it's a tough situation to be in.
Agree with B. Say that it has been difficult, but you'll figure it out.	
	Offer reluctantly: Ask if A needs help. Show that it would not be convenient indirectly. For example, say that you can rearrange your schedule.
MOVE 2: Recognize reluctance. Decline the offer by acknowledging B is busy. Say it's okay, you'll figure it out.	

⬅ ⬅ ⬅ ⬇	Confirm: Ask if A is sure.
Reassure B. Say you are sure. Talk about a different option you can try.	➡ ➡ ➡ ⬇
⬅ ⬅ ⬅ ⬇	Soften the implicit rejection and move toward a friendly close to the topic: Say you will help if nothing else works out.
MOVE 3: Acknowledge the gesture Thank B and move the conversation in a new direction.	

3. Practice. Work with a partner. Take turns being Partner A and Partner B. A makes sincere and insincere offers. B accepts or declines the offers.

Partner A	**Partner B**
SINCERE OFFER I can do it, no problem. No, I don't mind, not at all. I'd be happy to do it.	**ACCEPT OFFER** Wow, that's really great of you. I'm so relieved. I really appreciate it. You don't know how grateful I am.
INSINCERE OFFER Do you want me to help? I can move some things around if you really need me. Well, if you can't find anyone else, I guess I could . . .	**DECLINE INSINCERE OFFER** Oh no worries. I'll figure it out. Oh, don't bother. It'll be fine. I've got plenty of other possibilities. That's okay. It'll work out. It always does.

4. Plan. Develop a role-play using the moves in the instruction box on the previous pages.

c. Choose a situation from the box below or think of your own idea. Decide who will be **A** and **B**.

- **A** and **B** are former college roommates who live in different cities. **A** is visiting **B**'s city and would like a place to stay but does not want to ask directly.
- **A** wants **B** to go with her/him to shop for an outfit for a job interview.

- **A** is afraid to stay in a new apartment alone and wants **B** to spend the night.
- **A** needs help with homework and wants help from **B**.

d. Follow the moves and try different versions of having the conversation. For example, as **B** do not tell **A** whether you are sincere or not. Let **A** try to figure it out from your words and intonation and choose the best way to respond.

e. Practice your role-play, then perform your role-play for another pair. The other pair should guess whether the offer is sincere or not.

f. Watch another pair perform. Then discuss the experience. Would you use different words or ways of speaking in your first language? Explain.

ADDITIONAL PRACTICE

a. Close your books and practice the role-play without reading your notes. Listen to your partner and try to respond naturally.

b. Choose a new situation. Switch roles and repeat.

Assessment

Choose from the following assessments to reflect and give/get feedback on the experience. You can photocopy the forms in this book or go to http://www.alphabetpublishingbooks.com/integrated-skills-through-drama for downloadable versions.

TEACHER EVALUATION RUBRIC

<table>
<tr><td colspan="4"> Rising Water
 Actor's name: _____ </td></tr>
<tr><td colspan="4">Check all boxes that apply. Assign one score for each row. Add the two scores for a final score.</td></tr>
<tr>
<td></td>
<td>High 50–45
A pleasure to watch</td>
<td>Middle 44–35
Comfortable to watch</td>
<td>Low 34–0
Requires effort</td>
</tr>
<tr>
<td>Preparation & Performance

/50</td>
<td>☐ has memorized all lines
☐ speaks clearly with appropriate volume
☐ is believable in the role (pragmatics)
☐ responds to other actors realistically</td>
<td>☐ occasionally relies on script or prompting
☐ speaks so audience can hear
☐ is fairly believable in the role (pragmatics)
☐ attends to other actors naturally most of the time</td>
<td>☐ uses script
☐ speaks quietly or quickly so it is difficult to understand
☐ is not believable or breaks character, e.g., by laughing
☐ unnatural, inattentive, or unemotional response to other actors</td>
</tr>
<tr>
<td></td>
<td>High 50–45</td>
<td>Middle 45–35</td>
<td>Low 34–0</td>
</tr>
<tr>
<td>Language Delivery

/50</td>
<td>☐ conveys emotions through intonation and gesture
☐ uses effective sentence and word stress
☐ has clear pronunciation</td>
<td>☐ uses some intonation and gesture
☐ uses sentence and word stress most of the time
☐ has comprehensible pronunciation</td>
<td>☐ needs to work on intonation and gesture
☐ errors with sentence and word stress make comprehension difficult
☐ has pronunciation issues that interfere with comprehensibility</td>
</tr>
<tr>
<td>Total

/100</td>
<td></td>
<td></td>
<td></td>
</tr>
</table>

PEER FEEDBACK GUIDE

1. Ask another actor questions to learn more about their performance.

    a. What were your goals in creating your character and preparing for the performance?

    b. What did you enjoy about the process?

    c. What was hardest for you?

    d. Did you develop any skills? Explain.

2. Tell the actor about your experience watching the play. You may use the stems below or your own ideas.

    a. My impression was that your character felt . . .

    b. My favorite part was when . . .

    c. I'd like to know more about . . .

    d. The play made me think about . . .

SELF-REFLECTION

Actor's name: _____

Write three or four sentences explaining your answers to the questions below.

1. How did you prepare for your role?

2. Did anything happen that surprised you?

3. Did your language and/or conversation skills improve? Explain.

4. How do you feel about your performance?

5. What advice would you give to other actors?

Beyond the Classroom

HOST A PANEL DISCUSSION

How can society prepare for the challenges of the 21st century?

1. DISCUSS THE TOPIC. Form groups of three or four students. Each group take one question from below to discuss. Make sure everyone speaks. As a group, come up with three or four main points. Take notes. You will use these notes when you form a new panel.

Discussion Questions

Sign up for a question you are interested in and join a group. Also, feel free to change the questions or add new ones.

- ☐ **Group A:** What will the world be like when today's teenagers are adults? How will it be similar to or different from the past?
- ☐ **Group B:** What specific job or life skills will teenagers need in the future?
- ☐ **Group C:** How will education change to meet the needs of the 21st century?
- ☐ **Group D:** How much can teenagers be trusted to ensure that they mature in a healthy way? Give specific examples such as driving or going out at night.

Note: Some people will become moderators. Moderators introduce the panels and ask questions during the presentation.

2. RESEARCH. With your question in mind, reread the articles on teenagers and the future of cities. Also, gather more information about your group's question. Survey people in your community or go to an educational website on the Internet to learn more. Finally, think about your own experience as a teenager and with other teenagers.

3. WRITE A PAPER. Using your discussion notes and research, write a paper of three to five paragraphs about your question. You might find it useful to write one paragraph about each one of your major points. Use examples to make your ideas clear. Writing the paper will help you organize your information for the panel. Give and get feedback from other people with the same question.

4. PREPARE YOUR PANEL. Form panels that include one member from each group. Each panel should have someone from groups A, B, C, and D (If there are extra people, they can join an existing panel or form a smaller panel). Practice giving a two-minute talk based on your paper in the new group. You may use notes but to be effective, you want to talk, not read. Remember that stress and intonation are important for helping your audience understand.

Moderators: Choose one panel member to be a moderator. Discuss your role with the panel. You will explain the format of the panel, introduce each speaker, and ask questions. You will also invite the audience to ask questions. Don't be afraid of silence at first. If you wait, someone will usually come up with a question or comment.

Set a date and time for your panel discussion. Invite others from the community to attend if you wish, or present for classmates.

5. PRESENT. On the day of the presentation, have the panel members face the audience. The moderator introduces them and explains that each panelist will speak for one to two minutes about an issue affecting teens in the 21st century. Have each panelist talk for 2 minutes about his or her question. Try to speak directly to the audience without using your notes but cover all your major points. When all the panelists have spoken, the moderators should invite audience members to ask questions. Panel members then share their answers.

Sample Performance Day Schedule

Goal	Time	Activity
Warm-up	10 minutes	Cast assembles and sets up the stage.
Introduce Theme Critical thinking question	10 – 15 minutes	The director introduces a discussion topic, the critical thinking question of the play. The director invites students to do a pair-share about the following question. What changes can we expect to see in the next 20 to 30 years?
Prepare audience	1 minute	Director introduces the play and asks people to turn off their cell phones.
Performance	20 minutes	Cast performs the play and takes a curtain call.
Post-Play Talkback	10 – 15 minutes	Director passes out paper for small groups to prepare questions for talkback. Director facilitates the talkback in which audience makes comments or asks the actors questions.

Answer Key

DISCUSS THE TITLE

Answers will vary. Here are some sample answers.

1.

Who is talking?

A husband and wife.

Where are they?

At home.

What might have happened?

One of them used the credit card to make a big purchase, or they both have been spending a lot of money without realizing it.

2.

Who is talking?

Natalie's mother and her teacher.

Where are they?

At school, perhaps at a parent-teacher conference.

What might have happened?

Natalie, a student, is getting low grades because she isn't studying. She's spending her time on her cellphone or computer posting on social media, playing computer games or watching videos.

3.

Who is talking?

Two employees of a company.

Where are they?

At work.

What might have happened?

They were expecting to work together on a project, but it was cancelled. One may have expressed frustration with the other who defends herself because it was not her fault.

CONVERSATION SKILLS

Suggested Answers. Notice the person softens the statement to the person.

1. TO: Slow down. You're about to lose control of the car!

    ABOUT: Her driving was totally out of control. I thought I was going to die!

2. TO: Hey, hey, hey. That guy is out of control! Just walk away!

    ABOUT: It was all going okay, and then he just lost control and started a fight.

3. TO: I'm just saying. Your spending is a little out of control.

    ABOUT: He's completely lost control of his finances. I tried to talk to him, but I'm not sure it'll do any good.

4. TO: You can't go on like this. Your gaming is way out of control.

    ABOUT: He's gaming all day and all night. I think he's completely lost control! What are we going to do?

READ FOR BACKGROUND

Angry Oceans

Vocabulary

1. i.	2. j	3. h	4. b	5. d	6. a.
7. k	8. f	9. g	10. l	11. e	12. c

Discussion

Answers will vary. Here are some sample answers.

1. New Orleans is a famous American city that is built below the level of the sea. So it often floods when there are storms. The most famous example was in 2005 when Hurricane Katrina caused big waves that broke through the sea walls. Most of the city was underwater and it took years to recover.

2. I think the best ideas are to develop new technology that can stop global warming. Solar power and wind power are already happening in many places. I think it will be great if someone comes up with some new ideas though. We also need new technology to stop floods and tidal waves and protect cities from rising water. Maybe machines that clean carbon from the air can help.

3. My city is small, but there are many poor people. I think in 50 years, we will have some way to make cheap, but nice housing for poor people. I also hope there will be better transportation.

The buses in my city are ok, but they don't go to every place and they are slow. I hope we can get a subway or faster buses so people can go to work and other places easily. My city has a lot of nice beaches, but that means we could also get floods if the climate changes. So maybe we need to protect the city with big walls and people need to move away from the beach just in case.

HEROES OF THE STORM

Vocabulary

1. It was hard to understand what was happening completely

2. It made me feel emotional.

Discussion

Answers will vary. Here are some sample answers.

1. I would pack some clothes in a bag so that I am ready to leave the house. I would also call the police and try to find out what is happening. There are some places in our town that you can go if your house is flooded, like the schools or sometimes the YMCA. So I would try to be ready to go a place like that. And I would check if my neighbors need help, too. We all have to help each other when there is a big emergency.

2. I think that teenagers didn't have anything else to do because the schools were closed. And I think teenagers are young and strong, so they can work hard to move furniture or fix big things. They also have lots of energy. Teenagers like to have responsibility and to show that they are growing up. They are also members of a community, and they feel good about helping their neighbors.

3. I have had this experience in my life. When I was little, my father lost his job and it was very hard for him to find a new job. My mother wasn't working fulltime either, because she was taking care of me and my sister. So, we didn't have a lot of money. Until my father found a new job, we had to save. For six months, we had to eat only very cheap food. We bought chicken and rice for dinner every day or sometimes rice and beans and peanut butter sandwiches for lunch. We had no new clothes or toys or anything like that. When something broke, we couldn't get a new one. At first, my sister and I were very angry because we were hungry. Mom and Dad fought sometimes. Dad got angry that he couldn't find a new job. But after one month, Mom told us we are all together in this. And we have to be nice to each other. After that, we tried to always help Mom and Dad at home and we would never argue. We told Dad to cancel TV and Internet at home so we could read more books and play outside. It was fun. I think the hard times of being poor did bring out the best in us. Now my family still likes to talk together or read books instead of watching TV and my sister and I never ask for new toys or new anything because we appreciate the things that we have.

SHOULD WE FEAR THE TEENAGE BRAIN?
Vocabulary

1. b   2. a   3. b   4. b   5. a

Discussion

Answers will vary. Here are some sample answers.

1. When I was 16, my friends bought tickets to a concert in the city near my house. The concert was on a Thursday and I knew my parents would say I couldn't go because of school. So I decided to go without asking. We had to leave school early to get the train to the city. We went to the concert. My parents didn't know where I was. There were no cellphones then. The concert was a lot of fun, but I started to feel bad. I knew my parents would be scared and worried. So I found a pay phone and called them. My mom was very angry but she was also so happy I was alive and ok. She told me to finish the concert and come home. When we got back home, mom picked me up at the train station. She yelled at me so hard, but she also cried because she was so scared. I learned that I had hurt my parents very badly. I didn't think about how my parents loved me and cared about me. It was the first time I realized that my parents have feelings. After that, I never hurt or scared my parents again. Whenever I wanted to do something risky, I thought how will my parents feel?

2. My friend found out about a job as a manager in a university cafeteria. He wanted the job, so he applied and went to an interview. The person asked him a lot of questions about how he would solve different kinds of questions, and he tried his best to answer them. After a week, they offered him the job, but he didn't take it because he was afraid of all the problems.

3. I am very shy so I don't like to perform or talk to a lot of people. And I don't have a lot of money so I can't take financial risks. But I do like physical risks. My friends and I do lots of extreme sports, such as parkour. In this sport, you run through parks or other parts of the city, jumping over obstacles and climbing walls. Some people can even climb up buildings. I am not that experienced but someday I hope to be. It is a little scary for me because you can fall and really hurt yourself. Some people break their legs or arms. But the risk makes it fun.

DISCUSS THE PLAY

Answers will vary. Here are some sample answers.

1. Magnus is very organized and smart. I think he likes school and he gets good grades. He is preparing for a life in science or an area where following the rules and being smart is important. But maybe Magnus takes some risks in his academic work. For example, he says that he was talking about CRISPR, a way to control DNA. I think Magnus is very brave to try to learn about such a complicated subject.

Ajax is more like the teenagers we read about that like to take risks. Maybe he gets bored easily and he wants things to happen because he can't sit still. Like the article said, his brain may just need to have challenges in order to develop. Ajax is also confident about his physical skills in a way that Magnus is not. Ajax is sure that he can be a helper in a dangerous situation.

2. Ajax starts out feeling inferior and Magnus starts out feeling superior. How does this change during the play?

Ajax is not as organized and successful as Magnus so when they talk about taking a test and going to a job interview, Magnus is more prepared. But when the storm happens. Magnus is not able to help. He doesn't want to risk his life. Ajax is more impulsive, but also more successful during the storm. He saves his Dad and he also finds a boat to save his sister. Because he is brave, he is able to help people more than Magnus.

3. What mistakes do the adults in the play make? Why do they make them?

Gordon, Ajax's father, leaves the house to find Ajax even though he can't swim. Of course, he has to try to find his son during the flood. But it would be better for him to stay home. I think it shows how much he loves his son, but it also shows how Ajax is like him because both of them go out in the storm.

Sara, Ajax's mother, makes a mistake not to call emergency services earlier. They could have taken her and Ivy to the hospital or a safe place. Maybe they would have found Ajax, too. I think sometimes people don't realize that bad things can happen to them. She probably just waited too long. She was also worried about Ivy and didn't have time to think about the flood.

Mrs. Peele also never called emergency services on time. She was very busy helping everyone. But if she had called maybe they would have saved Sara and Ivy sooner and Ajax wouldn't have had to leave.

Maybe Petra made a mistake not to go with Ajax and trust him. After all, he was safe at the library, but her restaurant got ruined. I think like Sara, she didn't realize something bad could happen to her.

4. What kind of a person is Petra? How do you know?

She seems very nice, but not very brave. She just let Ajax go without helping him get to the library or get home. If it were me, I would have taken control of the situation and helped Ajax more.

5. What kind of person is Mrs. Peele? How do you know?

Mrs. Peele seems like a very nice person. She keeps the library open and feeds people and offers to make phone calls. She also keeps a positive attitude. She tells Gordon that everything is ok and that they will live through the storm, but it's hard for her to stay organized in a dangerous situation, so she fails to deliver the address to the emergency responders.

6. What is the message of the play? (What does it say about teenagers, risk-taking, and/or the future?)

I think there are many messages. The most important one for me is that sometimes a teenager who appears to be disorganized and impulsive can be a hero. The same characteristics that make Ajax a bad student, make him able to save his family. If Ajax thought about all the dangers, or waited until he had a perfect plan, he would never have left the library to find a boat to save his mother and sister. So his love of risk-taking and his impulsiveness end up being a big strength. It shows that we need all different kinds of people in the world.

LEARN YOUR PART

	Example one	*Example two*
accommodating	Chris does not eat meat, but she cooks meat dishes for her family.	The waitress allows a customer to substitute a salad for the French fries.
agitated	Kiki is biting her nails and walking up and down while she waits for the doctor to tell her whether she is sick or not.	A driver is stuck in traffic, and he starts honking his horn and yelling at other cars.
brainy	Raul takes the highest-level math and physics classes. He plans on becoming a rocket scientist.	A scientist studies genetic engineering, and he is able to cure diseases.
self-pitying	Ed tells his friends he has a terrible life because he has to use an old phone.	A student has a lot of homework, so he cannot go out with his friends. He complains that life is not fair.
ill at ease	Sven is not good at starting conversations, so he feels uncomfortable at parties.	Alice is not a very good dancer, so she usually stays at the table when people are dancing.
impulsive	Terry decides to climb a tree without thinking about how she will get back down.	Coral buys an expensive pair of shoes without thinking about her financial situation.
inferior	Tia was not invited to join the sports team. She's hurt, and it is hard for her to listen to others talking about it.	Hal bought a cheap watch, and now he's embarrassed about it.

	Example one	*Example two*
rebellious	Neda disobeys her parents and does not go to her Saturday math class. Instead she goes shopping with friends.	Pat refuses to wear a uniform at his job.
reckless	Li rides his motorcycle fast and does not wear a helmet.	Zach jumps off a high bridge into a river without checking the depth.
relieved	Wes's two-year-old daughter gets lost in a store. When Wes finds her, he is very happy she is safe.	Mrs. Smith forgets her phone on an airplane and the airline returns it to her.
reluctant	Dill wants to take the bus because he doesn't trust my driving. I argue that the bus will take too long, so he has agreed to go in my car if I promise to be careful.	Sue hates insects, so she does not want to go camping, but her friends convince her to come.
sarcastic	Rex says, "Good job!" when Sam forgets to bring the paperwork to the meeting.	Dmitri says, "Wow, that was a really good shot," when his friend misses the goal during a soccer game.
superior	Jen feels he should always sit in the front seat of the car because he is better than others.	Khalid always interrupts other students in class because he thinks his ideas are more important than others.

PRACTICING PRAGMATICS

2. Situations

A. 1. NS 2. S

B. 1. NS 2. S

SAMPLE ROLE-PLAY WITH A SINCERE OFFER

B: (*answering phone*) Hello?

A: Hi, B. It's A.

B: Oh, Hi A. How are you?

A: Good. Work is busy but it's not too bad.

B: Cool. How's Ali?

A: He's good, too. He says Hi. Look, I'm calling because I'm going to be in Boston next week.

B: That's awesome. Is this for work or fun?

A: For work. There's a big meeting between my bank and another bank.

B: Sounds important. Where are you staying?

A: Well, I haven't figured that out yet. You know, I don't know any of the hotels in Boston. I looked on the Internet, but the hotels are really expensive!

B: Well, why don't you stay with me? We've got plenty of room.

A: Are you sure I won't be in your way?

B: Of course not. It's no problem. We've got a guest room on the second floor and we even bought new sheets for the bed last week. Besides it'll be great to see you and catch up. When's the meeting?

A: Monday, but I'd fly in Sunday. I don't leave until Wednesday in case the meeting takes longer.

B: OK, perfect. Well, why don't I pick you up at the airport Sunday? And we'll go out to a nice place for dinner.

A: If you're sure it's ok.

B: It's ok. Email me your flight info, ok?

A: OK, I will. I really appreciate it.

B: Don't worry about it. See you next week!

SAMPLE ROLEPLAY WITH AN INSINCERE OFFER

A: Hi. What are you doing?

B: Nothing.

A: Good. Then you can come shopping with me.

B: Really?

A: Yeah, it'll be fun. And I need your advice. I need a suit for my interview.

B: You really want me to come? I don't know anything about professional clothes.

A: But you always look so put together.

B: That's because my mom buys all my stuff.

A: Oh, I should ask your mom!

B: You should! She's much better at this stuff than I am.

A: Too bad she's so far way.

B: Well, if you really, really need me, I'll go, but I'm not going to be much help.

A: Oh well, I don't want to force you.

B: It's not that. I just think someone else might be more helpful.

A: Yeah, maybe I can ask Sandy.

B: Sandy would be perfect!

A: Alright, I'll try her.

B: Good luck!

A: Thanks.

About the Author

Alice Savage comes from a family of theatre people. Her grandfather was a professor of theatre arts, and her father is a playwright. This drama background combined with a love of teaching has given her the opportunity to bring two passions together. In addition to *Rising Water*, Savage has also written *Her Own Worst Enemy* and *Best Intentions* for Alphabet Publishing.

Currently, a professor of ESOL at Lone Star College System, in Houston, Texas, she is grateful for the opportunity to spend time with young people who are facing the future clear eyes and strong hearts.